Disco
Wymondham
history
along its streets

by Anne & Adrian Hoare

Published by Anne and Adrian Hoare

By the same authors:

In Search of Robert Kett
On the Trail of Robert Kett of Wymondham
An Unlikely Rebel, Robert Kett & the Norfolk Rising
Standing up to Hitler, the Norfolk Home Guard & 'Secret Army'
The Wymondham Story
Looking back at Damgate
History along the Tiffey

First published 2012

ISBN   978-0-9574684-0-5

Printed by Barnwell Print Ltd.
Aylsham, Norfolk NR11 6SU
Tel: 01263 732767
www.barnwellprint.co.uk

WORLD
LAND
TRUST™
www.carbonbalancedpaper.com
Barnwell Print Reg. No. 2102

By using Carbon Balanced Paper
through the World Land Trust on this
publication we have offset 668kg of
Carbon & preserved 56sqm of
critically threatened tropical forests.

Carbon Balanced Paper. One of the most sustainable forms of communication that
will reduce your carbon foot print and promote CSR. www.carbonbalancepaper.com

Introduction

In the 1980s some members of Wymondham Heritage Society spoke to a number of elderly Wymondham residents. These conversations were taped. During the last two years, they have been listened to (many times !), transcribed and typed up. They provide important source material about Wymondham's history often revealing special knowledge and insights. A number of them talked about their childhood, school days, family, leisure time and work. Many of course, lived through both world wars. However it became obvious that these memories needed to be put into context for later generations.

This book uses their edited memories along with a wide range of other source material, to explore the town and reveal some of its stories through the lives of these people and many others and the buildings they lived or worked in.

Some of their memories provide links to other people and events in the town, which we have explored in more depth. In the process we discovered 'who lived where' in Wymondham, where they worked and how they earned a living – in some cases very precariously. We have tried to capture something of the spirit of a bygone age, in the process looking at parts of the town that have not featured in other publications.

We have taken a route along various streets in Wymondham to tell stories related to buildings, places and the people who lived there. Maps indicate that part of the town covered by each chapter. The origins of street names will be explained where this is possible. The book is not a guided walk. However, readers may find walking certain streets after this, will be a more enjoyable experience. Of course not all Wymondham's streets or houses are included. The book is neither definitive nor exhaustive. Damgate has been covered elsewhere !

Many of the photographs we have used are inevitably very old and therefore of indifferent quality. However this does not detract from their value as historical sources as they help to recall a bygone age. Many of the buildings appearing in this book no longer grace Wymondham's streets whose structure has changed little for centuries. But they have been very much part of the physical and social fabric of the town's story.

This book is based on over 30 years of study and includes information given to us at the Museum. By adding to the storehouse of knowledge about the town and giving it some shape and explanation, we hope it will increase understanding of Wymondham's history.

Those who had their memories recorded hoped their voices would be heard by future generations. By using many of these memories in this book, we have tried to make them available to a wider audience.

'History is the ship carrying living memories to the future.'
(Stephen Spender)

Chapter One
From Chapel Bridge to Melton Road

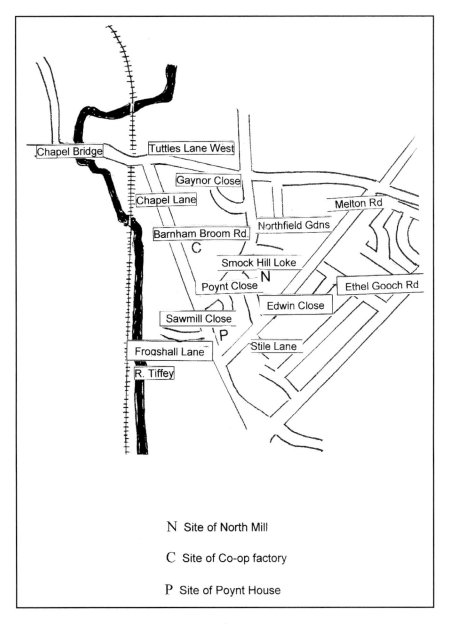

N Site of North Mill

C Site of Co-op factory

P Site of Poynt House

Chapel Bridge

There has been a bridge across the Tiffey at this point since early times. Its location on the western boundary of the parish of Wymondham was on the route into the town for travellers from Hingham, Watton and Swaffham. **Chapel Lane** gets its name from its link with the chapel on this bridge.

The bridge is named after the chapel founded by William d'Albini in 1145. He dedicated it to God and St Mary for lepers and 'impotent' people of the Order of Lazarus of Jerusalem. Offerings were collected from travellers by the master and two brothers who dwelt in the chapel, probably in return for using the bridge. There is a reference in 1455, to 'the reparation of the bridge of Westwade' in the accounts of Wymondham Priory which had built the bridge.

At the time of Kett's Rebellion in 1549, the chapel was owned by William Kett but after his demise, the bridge was forfeited to the Crown and then given to the Great Hospital in Norwich.

In 1722, the traveller and antiquarian Thomas Martin, visited Wymondham. During his stay he sketched the bridge and the ruins of the chapel on it, showing a footway at the side which was apparently wide enough for a horse too. By this time it was known as Westwade Chapel and belonging to the manor of Choseley.

In the mid 17th century the Quakers seem to have met illegally in the Chapel on the bridge at a time when only Anglican worship was permitted. However, after the Toleration Act of 1689, a new Quaker meeting house was built nearby.

During World War Two an evacuee family the Greens, lived in a small bungalow near the bridge opposite the Chapel Bell pub. The photo shows Mrs Green crossing Chapel Bridge with her three children in a cycle trailer, on their way to school along Chapel Lane.

One of Mrs Green's children wrote later, *'I look back on those days as some of the happiest in my life. My lasting memories are long days playing in the river and fields and riding to school on the bike trailer.'*

Mrs Green recalled the bungalow they rented; *'it was very small, kitchen, living room and one bedroom; we had no water or electricity but oil lamps and a stove and collected water from a well in the garden.'*

The present bridge is about 150 years old.

Poynt House – so called perhaps, because it is located at the point between Chapel Lane and Melton Road.

When this house was demolished in 1989, the Heritage Museum acquired a stone plaque and two patterned pammets with a rose and thistle on them. The inscription reads *'Watering Place, JP Harvey, Freehold 1833'*. The pammets came from a wall (dated 1831) comprising pieces of clinker, wood, iron, brick, flint and bottles, with a lime mortar. In White's Directory, 1836, Robert Harvey brick maker of Town Green was listed and a brick with Harvey inscribed

3

on its side was recovered from a wall at Poynt House. Two earlier references to a watering place have also been found.

The Harvey stone plaque

One of the patterned pammets showing the rose and thistle.

In 1637 John Barnard left his son his tenements and houses at *'the watery place'* near to *'Ton greene street'*. In 1761 Robert Sewell and his wife had the same property which was then described as two acres, one rood and a half of land called *'the Watering Close lying next to the King's Highway.....leading from Wymondham...towards Westwade Chappel'*.

Robert Semmence b. 1815, had founded the firm of Robert Semmence & Sons. It made wooden goods at his Cavick Saw Mills. After his death in 1893 his sons set up a sawmill and turnery at Poynt House which Robert had bought. William Semmence was living there in 1864, listed in White's Directory 1864 as a wood turner – Town Green.

Poynt House to the right of the Cock,
with the CWS chimney in the background

It was here that William set up his sawmills, later to become CWS (Co-operative Wholesale Society) Brush Works in 1917. His son George was still living there and running the business in 1900 – it is listed as Poynt Sawmills in Kelly's Directory 1900. Then a coach building department was set up there managed by George's son Herbert. In 1917 George sold the Poynt sawmills to the CWS of Leeds who used the sawmills to supply their Leeds brush factory with brush backs. Herbert carried on the coach building side for two years at Poynt House and then moved the business to Norwich Road. The demand for tumbrels, dog-carts etc declined with the increase in motor traffic.

After George Semmence, Poynt House was lived in by Arthur Pratt, chief cashier for the CWS Brushworks. Mr & Mrs Henry Halford, who started work at CWS in 1922, were the last people to occupy the house where they lived for 51 years.

George Semmence built Meadow View (no. 15 Chapel Lane) near the top of Frogshall Lane. Recently some decorated bricks or tiles have been found there, possibly brought by George Semmence from Poynt House.

Northfield House

Northfield House is one of the few properties in Chapel Lane which dates back to Victorian times.

In 1872 it was auctioned at the Green Dragon. According to the sale document it had a drawing room, dining room and morning room, five bedrooms and '*two excellent servants bedrooms*' on the second floor. '*A powerful force pump*' supplied water to the house which had a full-sized tennis lawn.

Northfield
House c. 1900

Northfield
House
in 1952

Frogshall Lane

This romantically named 'green lane' just off Chapel Lane, is shown on Faden's map, 1797. On the Enclosure Map of 1806, it is described as *'an ancient lane'*. 'Hall' in place names is usually derived from 'halh' – a sheltered place. Today there is just one house there, built on the site of a 19th century one.

In late Victorian times and the first half of the 20th century, in an era before political correctness, children had time to enjoy the countryside. One place which was a popular natural playground, was the meadow near Frogshall Lane, remembered fondly by many Wymondham residents.

Some memories of Frogshall and the meadow

Mrs Gladys White b. 1899 was born in the lane. She remembers *'two houses down there, now (1983) pulled down leaving old outhouses and half of one cottage – there's just the one bungalow now.'* She also recalls that there was no electricity or gas, *'only a well'*. She was still living in the lane at the time of the great Flood in August 1912, describing its impact as follows: *'it rose very quickly and the water covered the hedges and meadows and poplar trees disappeared under water and didn't come back for some weeks later. The railway line closed for several weeks.'*

Like most people of that time Mrs White lived a simple life –, *'we had nothing, but we were happy, we had an oven in the wall and had to get a fire going for a cup of tea. You could get a lot for a farthing. We had a box iron – you heated a piece of iron and then put it into the box in the iron. We always had a pig and chicken at Frogshall. My father used to get to Semmence's across the meadows – you could walk anywhere. In World War One, it was the only time the drains and rivers were cleared – it was done by POWS, splendid workers – nice fellows, Germans.'*

Mrs Cora Knighton b. 1898

She describes the lane as ' *a happy playground for children- we gathered acorns and sold them for 3d a bushel to Mr Shorten for his pigs. There was a delightful meadow there with a pond. Snipe flew over, there were frogs and toads in the stream which flowed down there where there was water cress. It was a happy hunting ground. Where Meadow View is now, there was a pond which froze over and we used to skate on it'.*

'Where the Co-op factory is now (1985) was a timber yard run by Mr George Semmence. He lived at Poynt House, and he built the house at the top of Frogshall, 'Meadow View' now no. 15, Chapel Lane. There were five cottages then, the bungalow, Meadow View and oak and sycamores down Frogshall Lane.

Sugar beet was first grown opposite the CWS factory by Mr Shorten. When they came to harvest it they had to get someone over from Holland to show them how to do it.'

The Co-operative Wholesale Society Brush Co (CWS)

The factory was on the Chapel Lane site for over 60 years. However the origins of this successful enterprise go back to the turn of the 20th century. About 1900 CWS was producing hand made brushes in London. In 1904 it moved to Leeds, where it was managed by a Wymondham man Mr A Saunders who re-organised, mechanised and enlarged the business which grew steadily.

In 1917 the CWS bought the Wymondham sawmills on the site from George Semmence. A small works employing six men was started; it supplied the Leeds factory with timber for brushes. One of the attractions of the area to such an industry, which Saunders would have known about, was the plentiful supply of timber. In 1922 it was decided to build a new factory here. It would have a 100 foot chimney, a water tower and boilers to produce the steam power to drive the generators making the factory independent for power supply.

The Co-op factory in 1948 – pole yards on far right

By 1932 production had doubled and with more sawmills it was cutting timber for wagon works, furniture, wringer rollers and even wooden kettle and iron handles and of course *good brushes for the millions'*. Apprenticeships were by now well established. An interesting product was the *'Samson non-slip deckchair.'*

In 1954 Mr R Bunn became manager – he re-organised and modernised the works. A new gantry sawmill was installed and a garden furniture section started. Apart from the chimney another memorable feature of the factory site were the pole yards where timber was stacked in readiness for conversion into a high quality product.

A wood ware department was re-organised and became very profitable. By the 1970s the factory was supplying not only to the Co-op market but also the trade in general. After Bunn's retirement in 1977, the factory lasted until 1983 – fierce competition made its position unviable. By then, its heyday when it employed over 300 people, was well over. When the factory closed it had less than 40 employees.

The main entrance 1988 – the iron railings which the company were unwilling to give up in wartime can be seen.

One of the last features to survive after closure, the factory chimney

The landmark chimney was finally brought down by controlled explosion in 1988. Incidentally, it was estimated that it contained 100,000 bricks and weighed nearly 400 tons Mr Bunn commented that *'memories will not be wiped out by the fall of a chimney.'*

Going, going, going, nearly gone ! the end of a landmark 1988

Now modern houses occupy the site where hundreds of skilled men and women worked for decades.

During World War Two, seven employees gave their lives. During the appeal for metal in 1942 the management said it was unable to hand over its iron railings at the front of the premises to the UDC as they protected their offices and works.

The CWS factory had been a very important part of the Wymondham economy and social life for over half a century. Employing over 300 people, it was second only to Briton Brush. It was also important for the innovations in the factory and the quality and range of its products with the *'invincible brushes'* for millions of homes together with furniture and goods for industry and agriculture.

In a town famous for its wood craft dating to medieval times, CWS embellished that tradition.

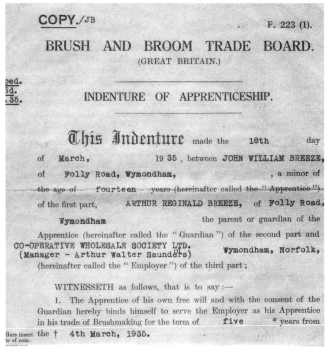

A reminder of training at CWS

Barnham Broom Road

Gaynor Close – Just after the road crosses Tuttles Lane, the first road on the right going toward the town is Gaynor Close. It was named after Dr G Gaynor a very popular and highly qualified physician and surgeon. By 1925 he had many responsibilities which included public vaccination officer for the district and medical officer for the Wicklewood workhouse. He was also Medical Officer to the Post Office and Board of Education and served as a certifying factory surgeon. He also served on the Urban District Council. Dr Gaynor used to visit his patients on a motor cycle. When he retired he gave money to make a bowling green in Priory Gardens. He died in 1967.

The Northfield Mill – known as the North Mill
There were originally three windmills in the town – one at Silfield another at Browick and this one, the last to disappear from the urban landscape in 1950.

This smock mill was first built in Lincolnshire and used as a marsh pumping mill before being moved to Dilham. Then in 1858 it was brought to Wymondham by rail. The mill had been bought by John Cann, farmer, millwright and brewer. Finding that nearby trees deprived the mill of sufficient wind power, it was raised another 14 feet, making it at 65 feet, the tallest smock mill in the county. The structure comprised seven storeys and was eight sided. The sails had a span of some 80 feet. The mill became one of the most prominent landmarks in Wymondham.

In 1883 it was bought by Henry King a miller and sawyer, who used it for steam sawing as well as milling. His descendants developed the steam sawing business into a furniture factory run by Henry Thomas King. This was along side the railway line – it had its own sidings, on the site now occupied by Aytons.

A sketch of the North Mill 1908

In 1935 William Farrow bought the mill, by now driven by an oil powered engine thereby removing the need for sails. Ten years later in 1945, it was sold to F.W. Myhill & Son, corn, cake, manure and seed merchants. Farrow described it as *'a powerful, old mill machine which did a lot of work'*.

In February 1950 fire broke out in the engine room and quickly spread. Five fire engines attended but were unable to save this historic mill. According to an eyewitness quoted in the EDP, ' *when the flames reached up to the sails they gave a last half turn before dropping into the burning mass of the mill below'*.

As a result of the activity of the fire brigade, half of the town was on low pressure and houses near the mill were practically without water. The Baptist Church house nearby was saved by the firemen.

The North Mill 1931

Smock Mill Loke nearby, is a reminder of the windmill.

The Heritage Museum has a stone slab with the inscription John Cann October 7th 1858, a reminder of one of the most prominent buildings in bygone Wymondham.

THE WINDMILL. WYMONDHAM

The mill some years before its demise in 1950

Melton Road

An important brick making area

Until c. 1700 flint, timber and clay lump were the most common building materials. But during the 18th century bricks and tiles were being made locally and soon replaced local materials and thatch. About 1826 two brick makers Robert Harvey, Town Green and Ann Watson, Northfield are known in the Barnham Broom, Melton Road and Pople Street area. The kilns are shown on Bryant's map. In 1907 Ransome's and Sharpe's had their entrance in Pople Street and Bidewells in Melton Road. They all continued production with Bidewells being the last to close in 1937. A hand drawn map dated c.1800 shows 'Mrs W's brick kiln' on the right side of Melton Road near the junction with Tuttles Lane.

A second kiln is shown between Melton Road and Pople Street. The 1907 Ordnance map shows the brick field between Melton Road and Pople Street and another on the left side of Pople Sreet and Hewitts Lane, opposite the entrance to Folly Road.

Several former residents of the town describe the brickworks – *'There was a brick kiln opposite the Rothbury* (Hewitts Lane) *and I went to see the bricks ready to be fired'* (Miss Lowe, daughter of Dr Lowe).

'Looking back up Pople Street... towards Folly Road was a stile which led to a windy path to a brick yard. This area was used for a council estate and all that remains is the gate and sign at the Melton Road end which directed the way to Stile Lane Veterinary surgery.' (Edith Carter).

Mrs Knighton recalled, *'The Brick Yard went on to the last war* (1939-45) *and the last house to be built of Wymondham brick was Westfields opposite the Abbey Church. Mr Marwood the engineer at Briton, had this house built.*

The brick yard was where the Vet is off Melton road – Mr Betts was the head and Mr Myhill and Mr Gooch worked there.'

In 1939 Molly Stone an evacuee from Gravesend, described being taken in with her sisters, by Mr and Mrs Myhill of the Brick Yard, Melton Road: *'Uncle Bert worked in the Mill (Northfield Mill) just up the road from the brick yard and we used to go and meet him from work.'*

Mrs Knighton also described how the bricks were made - '*Smoke would go up when they were firing bricks. They brought clay from fields along Pople Street on the left side. It was special clay and there was a quite a pit behind the drill hall in Pople Street. The clay was taken, mixed with sand and put in a big tub with paddles and shafting. A horse was attached to the shaft and went round and round turning a spindle. The mixed clay was then taken out and put in moulds. The kilns were fired with coal I think. There were long drying sheds with sides that let down so that air could get in. The bricks were laid out to dry in order. When they filled the kiln and fired it – one could come out a bit black sometimes. It went down a slope to a furnace underneath.*'

Greenhouses galore

In land between Barnham Broom and Melton Roads were two large areas of greenhouses belonging to two large nurseries. Charles Samuel Daniels & Sons were seed growers and nurserymen there in 1925.

The glasshouses were on the right of Barnham Broom Road, south of Northfield Gardens and on the left of Melton Road, north of Northfield Gardens. Hawthorn Cottage on Melton Road was believed to be the manager's house.

Glasshouses at Daniels Nurseries

The Northfield Gardens estate was completed by the Council in 1930-31. It got its name from the North Field – one of three large open fields in medieval Wymondham, divided into strips and shared out among the townspeople for cultivation.

The Friarscroft Laundry comes to Melton Road

In 1922 RC Rudrum wrote to the Council as follows: '*Having started a small hand laundry in Damgate, I now find that the premises are not large enough. I have therefore rented an old weaving factory in Friarscroft Lane....*'. The laundry in Damgate was believed to have been in Chalker's Yard, now demolished to make way for the Old People's Bungalows. Rudrum's letter marked the start of the Friarscroft Laundry. In 1926 it was converted to steam with its own water supply from a spring located in the meadow near the Tiffey.

In 1935 a new steam laundry was built in Melton Road and the laundry was transferred there.

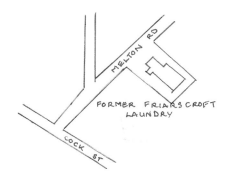

A number of Wymondham residents spoke of the manageress of the laundry, Una Chatterton who was a leading lady in many productions at the Town Hall. Originally working at Friarscroft as a secretary, she started off the laundry when it moved to Melton Road. She was a member of the Semmence family and displayed creative talent, through writing poems, singing and playing the piano.

Number 2, Melton Road – who do you think lived in this house ?

During the Second World War, Mrs Damsell, whose house this was, had a lodger Gerry Openshaw. He was a wireless operator who worked at the secret underground direction finding station located on the north side of Tuttles Lane East.

This Intercept station was one of nine in the British Isles. It consisted of a steel tank, 20 feet below ground with four vertical aerials above ground. These were all connected to the G.P.O. landline network at the centre of which was a special telephone switchboard and the plotting unit at Arkley View in Barnet, Herts. Access to the station was via a deeply recessed porch with a protective mound over it and down a ladder.

The secret underground station at Tuttles Lane, excavated and ready for removal after the war.

The work of the Radio Security Service was carried on in this underground station helping to track German spies who arrived here and were then captured. The main job was to find out what the Germans were thinking – all through the war. They listened to coded messages from the German Secret Service, Gestapo and the Secret Police. Operators like Gerry Openshaw could find out what Germans believed our intentions were and what they knew about our plans for the invasion of Europe. By sending false signals, the Germans were led to believe that the D Day landings in 1944 would be in the Pas de Calais **not** Normandy.

Another operator, a Welshman, was very popular in Wymondham, because he mended everyone's radios ! But no one knew of his secret life like Openshaw's, who played a very important part in the defeat of Germany.

Chapter Two
From Cock Street to Vicar Street

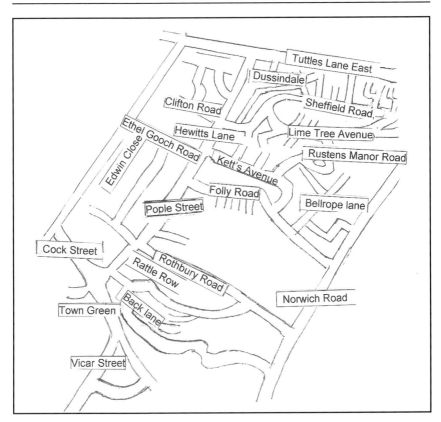

Cock Street

Number 22, known as Trafford House, on the corner of Melton Road, was occupied in the late 19th century by the Dunham family. Mrs Knighton said that they called it Dunham's Hill. The Dunham's started a hand laundry there in the 1890s which in due course was taken over and eventually became the Wymondham Laundry in Norwich Road.

Dunham's House is also mentioned in a list of 19th century 'Bower Houses' where according to ancient custom, beer could be served without a licence on Fair Days in the town. There was also a small section of a maltings there.

Numbers 18 & 20 – these two properties were occupied as one house for over 40 years before being sold in 1918 by the Glasspoole family. The head of the household, Arthur Glasspoole could be described as a 'Renaissance man' because of his many talents. He was a solicitor's clerk, music seller and teacher, organ builder, Registrar of Births, Marriages & Deaths for the Wymondham sub-district, auctioneer, Inspector of Nuisances for the Rural Sanitary Authority, Secretary of the Wymondham Gas Co., Sanitary Inspector for the Hundred of Forehoe, Valuation Officer for Wymondham and clerk to the Lighting Authority. He also found time to serve as Wymondham Abbey organist from 1867-1880.

Cock Street in 1912 at the time of the great flood. Numbers 18 & 20 can be seen on the right, second property from the end

Gladys White thought the Glasspooles were *'a very interesting and clever family'. They all played a musical instrument and would be heard playing at home on Sunday afternoons. Mr Glasspoole was definitely the boss !'*

Arthur Glasspoole built a chapel at the end of his garden where he and his brother built and repaired organs around 1878. Despite a fire in 1902, pieces from other old buildings, organ pipes, church furniture and music remained there until the 1970s. In 1911 a Roman Catholic evangelising mission, sent by the bishop of Northampton, came to King's Head Meadow. Cecil Cross a Wymondham cabinet maker, was an early convert. Due to his connection with Arthur Glasspoole, a Roman Catholic church was set up in the chapel built at numbers 18-20 Cock Street. (See photograph).

Mass was said for the first time by Fr. H G Hughes, in January 1912. Arthur Glasspoole played the organ. The chapel was served from St John's Norwich and services were held on alternate Sundays at 10 am and every Wednesday at 7pm. These details were still advertised in a 1925 directory.

Mr Glasspoole had also extended his property, numbers 18-20, in 1879, but now it is two separate houses.

Number 16, the Merchant's House, is an exceptional mid Tudor former merchant's house c. 1545.

In 1912 as 'the Chestnuts', it was the home of a more recent Wymondham merchant, Edward 'Ginger' Clarke. He opened Clarke & Co at the corner of Market Street and Damgate. This popular draper's and grocer's shop was founded in 1871 and continued until 1970 just after the death of his son Harry in 1969. The site is now occupied by Geo. R Reeve.

The Cock Inn

The former inn which gives the street its name was timber framed and originally thatched. It dates to at least the 17th century. An adjoining cottage and shop owned by the brewers Cann & Clarke was partly incorporated into the pub in the late Victorian period. In 1894 it was included in the sale of Wymondham Brewery to Morgans. In 1996 it was sold by Phoenix Inns to a private buyer.

The Cock Inn 1884

'Blank House'

The part of Applegarth fronting on to Cock Street was built where the house and grounds known as Blank House was located. Its long wall and shrubs, which can be seen on the left in the next photograph, just beyond the two children, faced Cock Street. Thomas Edward Auger was the Vet and Inspector of contagious cattle diseases for Forehoe, who worked from this house in 1878.

By 1925 another vet, Harry Standley had taken over the premises.

Unicorn House on left, with two children outside

Unicorn House

According to E B Pomeroy working as a solicitor in Vicar Street in 1878, Unicorn House (see above), was a *'Bower House'* where alcohol, according to ancient tradition, could be served without a licence on Fair Days. As Unicorn House it was the home of the Wymer family. Cora born in 1900, whose married name was Knighton, has left memories of Wymondham life in the 20th century.

Alfred Wymer, Cora's grandfather, had his wheelwright's business there in 1883, but by 1912 William, her father had taken over. He died in 1945.

Some of Cora Knighton's memories of the business:

'I was born in this house; I never saw my grandparents much but they left six houses which have been modernised. One of the deeds says "because of the love and affection that my son William and I have for each other, I sell him the business for 10 shillings."'.

Cora Knighton with friends at Becket's Well Bridge, 1920s

'*Dad and granddad were wheelwrights and carpenters. A photo of Unicorn House showed the name A Wymer, wheelwright and carpenter, under the window. The house next door to us, pulled down now, was a tannery; this yard was known as the tan yard. Mr Auger the vet bought it in 1894.*'

'*Dad would never make his perfectionist business pay today. He would get a fir tree long enough to make a 54 stave ladder, start at one end, saw the pole in half and would not be a tenth of an inch out. He used to varnish pony traps and mend wheels and decorate them, using a brush with 4 inch bristles and made a perfect round.*
'*The business was hit after World War One. After Woolworths came to Wymondhan, farmers could buy nails, paint and do their own work like making gates – also carts were going out of use. So Dad worked for Aytons repairing tumbrels and making wheels for them. Mum and I helped Dad turn the treadle lathe. Although he had two apprentices, he had to let them go and carry on on his own. I loved to see him turn a rough piece of elm into a hub with beading – there's one in the Heritage Museum.*

Dad took the wheels to a blacksmith for spokes on a handcart. 'Wood was kept in the top shop. We had the old saw pit, the only one left in the town. A man at the top and one at the bottom would saw their own planks. You could buy them from George Semmence's wood sheds across the road or Alfred at Becket's Well. Dad always wrote down what he got because you would just get a bill to goods.'

Town Green

By the 12th century Wymondham was comprised of three parts. There were settlements around Town Green, the Market Place and the Priory and Becket's Chapel.

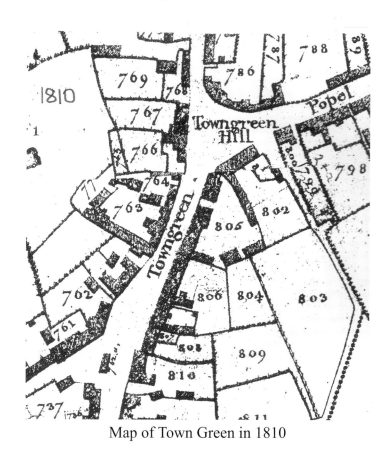

Map of Town Green in 1810

Tuddenham's & Wharton's butchers
Now occupied by Merv's bakery, Tuddenham's had been a butchers here from at least 1883. John Wharton took over in 1914 after the death of William Tuddenham. Wharton already had a shop in Damgate and the two continued until 1938 when the business moved to Market Street.

Wharton's butcher's in Town Green

Mrs Eva Chapman a Wymondham resident, recalls the Town Green shop - '*I can remember the first world war and seeing a Zeppelin. I was told to go indoors as it would be safer. My mother lived at the Town Green butcher's shop which my father had bought in 1914. We had soldiers billeted there – the drawing room was for sergeants and the harness room for privates! Opposite the butchers was Laycock's drapery and grocery business.*
At first we had no fridges but I remember the first one at Town Green run by ice, delivered from Norwich twice a week and put in a tank at the back. Mother put custard in and made ice cream'

'*Mother would make pork cheese in a huge iron boiler and cook tongue. Mum and Dad made huge bowls of dripping with lovely brown gravy in the bottom. I would be sent to take some to poor families in Culyer's Yard and Rattle Row. The husbands were in work but earned little. They were customers who might come in for two pennyworth of bones. They also had scraps when pork was rendered down, cut into one inch squares and came out hard and crisp. You got a lot for 2 d and they were very tasty.'*

The house next to Whartons
The premises next to Merv's bakery going towards the town had a fireplace with large dressed stones taken from the demolished Abbey buildings.

Part of the brick fireplace showing the stones from the Abbey incorporated in it.

Leather Bottle
To the left of Whartons, was the sign for Young's, Crawshaw & Young's brewery attached to the wall of the Leather Bottle pub next door. The pub dates to the 18th century.

The story of the 'One Stop' shop

'One Stop' was once the grocer's, draper's and outfitter's shop of J
R Smith & Son established in 1857. Incidentally he was also listed
as a *'brick and tile maker'*. He sold everything from provisions to

hats and coats and presumably bricks! The shop closed in 1911 on
the death of J R Smith's son William.
CG and EG Atherton also traded as provision merchants near this
shop. Eva Chapman talks about Mr Laycock's grocer's and drapery
opposite Wharton's butcher's shop, where she lived.

In 1964 Herbert Corston moved here from his shop in Damgate and
traded as Mace Stores.

The shop next door, now the Shapla Tandoori restaurant, was
Plunkett's greengrocers in 1912. From 1864 to the 1880s,
Emily and Adeline Poll were grocers and drapers in the same

group of premises. Poll's Yard, a yard of small cottages just beyond Shapla presumably got its name from them.

Plunkett's greengrocer's shop c. 1910

Pople Street perhaps named after the poplar trees which once grew along it.

R Shorten & Sons

Where India Village is now, was the Model Bakery belonging to Bob Shorten. He started his business in Pople Street in 1906 where Woodbine's Fish & Chip shop was. He was a great character and a well known preacher who also made political speeches for the Liberal cause. One of these began, '*Now friends – imagine we are electing a Board of Directors. Who shall we have ? Ramsay Macdonald – he's no good ! Stanley Baldwin – what's he smoke ? Honeydew (tobacco) – all honey and no do !'*

Edith Carter, daughter of a Master Brush Maker

Edith recalls interesting stories of Town Green folk enjoying simple pleasures, childhood fun and living at a brush works. Her father began hand brush making in Market Street (1909) and had to wait until the licence of the Dove public house in Pople Street expired (1912) before he moved the business there.

Pople Street during the 1912 Flood – poplar trees on left

At one time William Carter employed nine workers. Incidentally, in the garden of this property small oak trees were grown from acorns collected from Kett's Oak.

Edith's memories give an important insight into the social life of the town.

The former Dove public house

'I lived all my life in the same house which stood in Town Green, but some years ago it was transported to Pople Street. Opposite the Dove lived Bob Shorten the baker (now India Village). *The Dove had a thatched roof until 1895. Father used to pass it on the way to the Commercial School at the Rothbury in Hewitts Lane.'*

Childhood fun

'Our little corner had always been referred to as 'Town Green Hill'. I spent many happy hours watching films, concert parties and pantomimes accompanied by a small orchestra in the Town Hall'. (the site is now a commercial premises). *What is now part of the Indian restaurant, was Mrs Felstead's lending library. It was a 1d a week. I was sometimes sent to fetch a book for mother. Mrs Felstead would say "I've got a new book by Densy Robbins". When we realised the author's name was Denise, we had a little giggle outside.'*

'It was exciting to be sent to the corner shop for 'fancy' biscuits and hope that they would have to open a new tin – no packets then – as there would be one of each kind of the lovely selection. We could also buy a pennyworth of coconut weighed into a pointed sweet bag.'

'As children we loved to hang around the workplace and our favourite thing was the upper part of the workshop. Here women were setting knots in the brush handles by first dipping them in boiling pitch. They had a lump of chalk to rub on their fingers to stop the pitch sticking to their skin and we would beg for bits of this to use on our blackboards.'

Living with brush making

The bustle of her father's brush making business is captured in the following memories:

'On the ground floor was a small engine which drove the machine boring holes in the brush and broom backs. Every few days a big delivery cart of the LNER railway would pull into the yard, drawn by a huge horse carrying sacks of Chinese bristles and other materials. We liked these because they were packed in tea chests which made splendid boats to journey to distant lands with broom handles for oars ! Sometimes we made a stage from the boxes. Materials came from China, India and Mauritius. Bristles for shaving brushes were sterilised. The best

artists' brushes were made of sable. Nail, scrubbing, laundry, shaving, hair, shoe, clothes, hat, crumb, bottle, cobweb, paint, distemper, stove and soft and stiff sweeping brushes and brooms were made at my father's works.'

Carter's brush making business faces economic changes

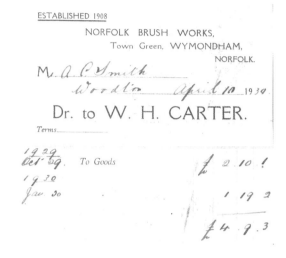

'Eventually machines dominated the manufacture of these items and people were less inclined to pay for hand made ones. Father was not prepared to launch into this and his workers drifted away to Britons or CWS. The old workers would sit and sing while they worked.'

Stories about some of Edith's neighbours

Granny Woodbine – *'she was never without an apron, man's cap and plimsolls. She'd left school at ten, never learned to read and write and worked in fields picking stones. She always bought a daily newspaper because she like to read the 'gailies' – Norfolk for pictures.'*

Brian Wigg and his sister, no. 5 Town Green - *'He was a retired schoolmaster and keen naturalist who rarely returned from his daily walk or drive with Dr Buckton without some leaf or flower to study through his microscope. He often talked to my father and once presented him with beautifully drawn illustrations.'*

Percy Andrews

'In the 1920s Percy Andrews assembled early wireless sets. He acquired a loudspeaker while we were listening with earphones. He would place the loudspeaker on the windowsill so that people could listen in. One evening a concert was announced to be relayed from 2LO Radio and out floated the voice of Mavis Bennett the famous soprano. Among the gathering of those listening was George Clarke, nicknamed 'Beach' Clarke, an old sailor who rocked back and forward on his feet as if on board a ship. When someone remarked how wonderful it was to hear the voice coming from 100 miles away, he retorted that it wasn't coming from London, but it was a woman singing, because he saw her go in through the front door !'

A changing street scene in Pople Street

'Looking back up Pople Street on the right, one remembers that two clay lump cottages were demolished and replaced by numbers 24 and 26. Almost opposite were two more clay lump cottages replaced by 'The Chestnuts'.

Pople Street, with the Dove on the left. Shorten's bakery was on the right. The poplar trees can also be seen clearly .

35

Rattle Row

Further along the road on the right was a terrace built in 1810-1820 to house local weavers It took it name from the noisy *'clackity clack'* of the looms of the weavers who lived and worked in these small cottages.

By the 1830s there were over 600 weavers in Wymondham. But decline had set in by the 1840s with the coming of the Industrial Revolution and steam powered machinery in northern England. A major depression in weaving followed and unemployment rose.

Rattle Row (below), remained as a symbol of the weaving era. It was sadly demolished in 1977, despite a vigorous campaign to save it by the Wymondham Society. An old people's bungalows complex was built on the site which once echoed to the sound of skilled and industrious Wymondham weavers.

The Drill Hall

On the opposite side of the road is the Drill Hall. In the peace celebrations of July 1919, there was a united service, rural sports and a dinner served in the Drill Hall by the Welcome Home committee.

The celebration dinner in the Drill Hall

The Rothbury

Further along on the right at the junction with Rothbury Road is a substantial house, the Rothbury.

It had a dark secret. Thomas Mays a veterinary surgeon had a horse shoeing business and employed two men in their fifties, Henry Bidewell and Henry March. A quarrel broke out between the two men to do with Mays giving up the business. In the ensuing fight March killed Mays and Bidewell with an iron bar. He was hanged at Norwich Castle in Nov. 1877. A public fund was set up to support the families of Bidewell and March. The tragedy caused much distress and March's family changed their name.

In 1886 the Rothbury was opened as the Commercial School – it survived until 1898 and for a short period provided an alternative to the town's grammar school and competition on the sports field.

A group of masters and senior boys at the Commercial School

The school was founded as a middle class school to provide at minimum cost, a sound education to the sons of tradesmen and the like.

After the school closed, the Rothbury became a private house – it had seven main rooms, five bedrooms and servants' quarters, also extensive outside premises, gardens, orchard and kitchen garden. It was sold in 1919.

In 1994 it was offered for sale again as a development site with the house, cottage, building plot and barn in tree lined grounds.

On the right of Pople Street, off Folly Road is:

Sir Thomas Beevor Close
Beevor was a leading figure in the building of Wymondham Bridewell in 1785. He also drew up rules for this new *'model*

prison', based on the ideas of prison reformer John Howard. The Bridewell influenced prison design and the treatment of inmates in other parts of the country and America.

Hewitts Lane

Just after Pople Street becomes Hewitts Lane, on the left is **Ethel Gooch Road** named in honour of Ethel Gooch wife of Edwin. Like her husband she was a staunch Labour Party supporter. She was the first woman to be chair of the Urban District Council and became a distinguished figure in public life both in Wymondham and Norfolk.

Edwin Close
Son of a blacksmith in Fairland Street, Edwin Gooch was a founding father of the Wymondham Labour Party. He became political agent to George Edwards who was elected as the first Labour MP for South Norfolk in 1920, the first working man from Norfolk to win a seat.

MR. G. EDWARDS M.P. WITH HIS AGENT. AFTER THE COUNTING 2118 MAJORITY.

Edwin became President of the National Union of Agricultural Workers, and Labour MP for North Norfolk from 1945 until his death in 1964 He also served on the Labour Party Executive, becoming chairman of the Labour Party in 1955-56.

Gooch on the left, with George Edwards after the by-election victory in 1920.

It is appropriate that both Ethel Gooch Road and Edwin Close, on a Wymondham council estate, were named after such vigorous champions of the working class. Incidentally Ethel served on a government advisory body for the design of dwellings.

Further up Hewitts Lane on the left is:

Robert Kett School
The school is named after Wymondham's most famous son, leader of the Norfolk Rising (1549) against the enclosure of common land and other social injustices. Each year pupils lay flowers at the plaque placed on Becket's Chapel in 1999 (the 450th anniversary of the rebellion), in memory of Kett and all those who died in the cause he championed.

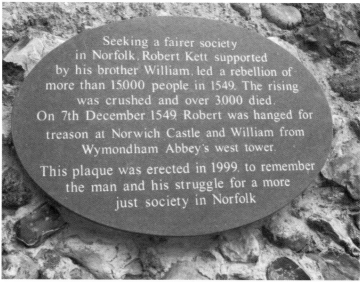

Kett's Avenue and Kett Close on the opposite side of the road were named in honour of a local hero.

Further along Hewitts Lane on the right, off Sheffield Road and Lime Tree Avenue, are a group of roads whose names echo people and places in the story of Kett's Rebellion.

Dussindale

This is the name of the final battle in Kett's Rebellion. The rebel army was defeated by a large royal force on 27 August 1549. 3,000 of Kett's followers died and the Kett brothers were captured after the battle. They were taken to London where they were found guilty of treason. Then they were brought back to Norfolk for public execution.

Mount Surrey

A lavish house built by Duke of Norfolk's son on Mousehold Heath. It was sacked and occupied by the rebels who used it to imprison captured members of the Norfolk gentry.

Warwick Drive

The Earl of Warwick was the royal commander who defeated the rebel army at Dussindale.

Sheffield Road

The Earl of Sheffield was the deputy commander to the first royal army sent to Nowich against the rebels on 31 July 1549. He was killed in the fighting near St Martin's Plain.

William and Robert Close named after the Kett brothers Robert and William. William was a loyal supporter throughout the rebellion. He was eventually hanged, from the west tower of the Abbey church on 7 December 1549.

Conyers

Tom Coniers was a minister at St Martin Church in Norwich, but became chaplain at Kett's camp on Mousehold Heath.

Oak Close

There were two oak trees in the area connected with the rebellion. *'Kett's Oak'* just outside the town on the B1172. It was the starting point of a great protest march to Norwich against the injustices of the day. It was led by Kett who it is believed, made a stirring speech at this oak.

The other oak tree in the story, known as the 'Oak of Reformation', was on Mousehold Heath. It became the centre of government at the camp. Trials of corrupt gentry were held there as Kett listened beneath the oak. The tree no longer stands.

This image is taken from Ashburton's History, 1793. It shows Kett under the *'Oak of Reformation'*, presiding over a trial of a member of the Norfolk gentry.

Hobart Close
Master Hobart was a Morley landowner who had enclosed common land in the village. His fences were pulled down by angry peasants who had been stirred up by drink- fuelled talk at the Wymondham Fair in July 1549.

Steward Close
Augustine Steward was Deputy Mayor of Norwich after Mayor Codd had been captured by the rebels. Augustine Steward took over the administration of the city. He received both royal commanders in his house in Tombland, where there was much street fighting in the last days of the rebellion.

Abbot Close
A reminder of the centuries when there was a thriving monastery in the town whose Abbot was one of the most important figures in the area. Originally a priory it was granted independent status as an abbey in 1448.

St Leonards Close opposite side of Hewitts Lane
Site of a former priory on Mousehold Heath, it was acquired by the duke of Norfolk after the Dissolution. His son the Earl of Surrey built his house Mount Surrey, on the site.

Clifton Road
Sir John Clifton supported the campaign by the townspeople to build the great west tower for the church. The octagonal east tower symbolised the former monastery.

Arundel Drive
The second William d'Albini was created earl of Arundel by King Stephen.

Town Green again

The Feathers
Once known as The Three Feathers. From the early 1900s it was the Prince of Wales Feathers. The property dates from the 18th century. In 1776 it was advertised for sale in the Norwich Chronicle and the records show that the house included a slaughterhouse.

In 1877 Henry March, the notorious murderer, had his last pint here before he was arrested and later executed for the murder of Thomas Mays and Henry Bidewell at the Rothbury.

An early photo of the Feathers c. 1900 – the sign is of large Norwich brewers, Steward & Patteson

Numbers 9-11, Town Green

Numbers 9-11 Town Green were occupied by the printing works of Geo. R Reeve Ltd. The oldest part is jettied and of at least 17th century origins or earlier. The timber frame is exposed inside and has traces of a wall painting. The subject is hard to decipher but is possibly heraldic.

The earliest document to come to light dates from 1751 when the property was sold to Thomas Harvey, baker and maltster and later Zachariah Spottiswood Browne, a wealthy tanner.

In 1816 it was acquired for £2,250 by Thomas Cann the Younger, described as a miller and a member of the brewing family. The malthouse, kilns, granaries and storerooms were occupied by Mr Cann and the yard was shared by all the occupiers of the cottages and malthouse.

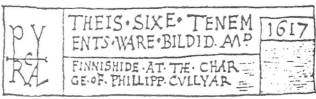

In this yard, known as Cullyer's Yard were the six almshouses given by Philip Cullyer to the town to replace those *'decayed in the fire'* (John Wilson), which bore the inscription copied by Thomas Martin in 1712. They were bought by Mr Standley in the late 19th century. The almshouses were still lived in by local people in the 1950s but by 1960 they had been demolished.

In 1901 the premises were sold to Henry Girling Stone who moved his printing business there. The property comprised five cottages and a shop. Stone refaced and rebuilt some of them naming them Caxton Villa. In 1937 the Methodist Church was offered Caxton Villa as a manse and it was renamed Stoneleigh in memory of his generosity. In 1969 when the church wanted to build a new manse, Stoneleigh was bought back for the business. When Stone's closed in 1992, Brian Seager, managing director of Geo. R Reeve, printers, moved his business there in 1994.

Part of Stone's the printer, the first property on right

3, Town Green

The **Little Dustpan**, an iron mongers, was founded in 1886 by Charles Harvey Standley. Deliveries were made within a six mile radius by horse and cart and later a van. The shop continued to be run by the Standley family until 1988 when Philip and Pamela retired. The site is now occupied by the Antiques and Collectors Centre.

The frontage of the Little Dustpan, early 1900s

In its later years the Little Dustpan sold cycles, radios and televisions. Petrol pumps were added in the 1930s but removed in 1966.

Number 1, Town Green – the Town or Public Hall

The foundation stone of Wymondham's first Town Hall was laid in 1888 by Mr E B Pomeroy. The spectators include grammar school boys in the front.

The completed Town Hall - the site is now occupied
by various businesses.

This building, often referred to as the picture palace as it was the
cinema in Wymondham before the Regal opened, was used for
a variety of entertainments. For many residents a visit was the
highlight of the week. **Mr W G Wilson** recalls visits as a boy to see
films in the early 20th century:

*'The old picture palace in Town Green was run by Mr Spalding
and Miss Reeve the sister of George Reeve the printer. She played
the piano with tunes to coincide with the antics of Charlie Chan,
Charlie Chaplin, Harold Lloyd and Pearl White. I had to clean my
mother's cutlery to earn a few pence to go to the Saturday afternoon
show.'*

Mrs Knighton was another resident who had vivid memories of
the entertainment there:
'Una Chatterton was a leading light in Wymondham theatricals.

Archdeacon Collier's wife was very keen on drama. I started my life on the stage at the Old Town Hall. There were men's and lady's dressing rooms and Mrs Collier arranged tableaux with my sister and I as gipsies. The Colliers left Wymondham in 1911.'

'Then there was the Wymondham Amateur Theatrical Society WATS: Curate Rev Oakley wrote the first panto – Russell Bartram was in the orchestra, Mr Musto was conductor, 1926 – 8. There was also a Choral Society in 1926 – the conductor was known by choir boys as 'Whisky Wilde'. He walked from Norwich and played the organ at church, had lunch at the Green Dragon and walked back to Norwich in the evening. In Hiawatha's Wedding feast he fixed up for a tenor from King's College to sing a solo.'

A production of the Pirates of Penzance
at the Town Hall, early 1900s

In 1935, 400 children queued for the annual treat in the Town Hall, given to them by the Wymondham British Legion

A new role for an old building

In March 1944 the Anglo American Services Club (see next photo), opened in the Old Town Hall and picture house, as it was often called. It was run by the Church Army The club gave opportunities for American and British servicemen to socialise in its canteen, recreation rooms and dance area.

Pamela Standley met airmen form Deopham Green and Hethel and staff from the American Army hospital at Morley, in the Church Army Canteen (CAC) there.
There seems to have been a high level of supervision! She recalls:
'I went to the 'Open House' at Morley on Sunday afternoons. We met outside the CAC at Town Green and we were chaperoned (I think that would be the word) by Mrs Pratt of the British Red Cross.'

The Yeoman's House

This was formerly known as Cullyer's House, a splendid 17th century property belonging to Philip Cullyer, a prominent figure in the town. After the Great Fire of 1615 which destroyed the first Market Cross, the town was financially hard pressed to make good certain public buildings. But by 1617-18 the new Market Cross had been completed with the aid of £25. 7s. loaned by Philip Cullyer. Today the house comprises **numbers 14, 16, 18 & 20**. Cullyer's almshouses opposite are now gone.

The Wymondham Workhouse (on the site of Methodist Church)

In the 16th and 17th centuries the government faced a big social problem with the growing numbers of poor people who could not be provided for by their own families. However, Wymondham had a number of 'town houses' in which poor people could live free of charge or on a low rent. But they were expected to work for their keep.

By 1619 the local JPs had set up a **Bridewell,** or house of correction, where those who would not work for their relief, were *'set on work'.* But this left paupers who needed somewhere where they could be supervised in their work. The needs of this group worsened in the 1620s as a result of a trade slump, plague and poor harvests. By 1621 in Wymondham some were near to starvation and several hundred in dire poverty. This represented a substantial part of the population.

In 1631 local JPs ordered a **workhouse** to be set up in two town houses in Town Green 'to set to work' the homeless poor at spinning. It became a small twisting mill which was maintained at the town's expense.

By the 1820s Wymondham was producing bombazines and crapes for mourning clothes. Cornelius Tipple had a small factory which operated in the former workhouse in Town Green.

Pulling down the old workhouse to provide a site for the
Methodist Church, 1869

The Methodist Chapel

The Methodist Chapel was designed by Mr Edward Boardman of Norwich for 500 people. It opened in May 1871 at a cost of £1,248. The site had been bought by J R Smith, who had a grocery and drapery at the junction of Town Green and Pople Street. He paid £300 for it in 1870

PRIMITIVE METHODIST CHAPEL, WYMONDHAM

The War Memorial

This stands at the junction of Town Green and Vicar Street, on a triangle of land near the Town Hall, given to the town by Mrs Cautley of Abbotsford in Vicar Street. It was unveiled and dedicated on 25 July 1921 in the presence of ex servicemen, families of the dead, VAD nurses, cadets, boy scouts, girl guides, churches and other groups. Major Cautley presided and the service was led by the Rev Martin-Jones, Vicar of Wymondham. It honoured the memory of the 142 men of Wymondham who lost their lives in the Great War of 1914-18.

The War Memorial was built on the site where railings and shrubs can be seen on the left of this photo

Early photo of the War Memorial; Rook House is 3rd on right

Vicar Street

Vicar Street has the look of a small cathedral close and has probably changed little since the early 19th century. The street got its name because the vicarage has always been located here near the Abbey Church.

Number 8, Rook House

This house was one of the properties burnt during the Great Fire of 1615. (See photograph on page 53).

When was the house built ?

Rook House, was surveyed in 1986 and described as a timber framed seven bay, lobby entrance house, with a cart entrance to the south and some mullioned windows. It was tentatively dated to the first half of the 17th century.

In the 18th century the lower walls were thickened, obliterating the jetty. The lower front elevation was given sliding sash windows. The central chimney is cut through from the front to the rear of the house forming an arched passage, as in the former White Hart in Market Street.

Recently a contemporary forgery of a copper alloy farthing of Charles I, dating 1625-34, was found in the excavation for a drainage connection in the passageway for Rook House and may give a clue to the construction date.

Was Rook House the Guildhall ?

In 1621 a survey of Wymondham and Aylsham (St Peter's), with a *'noate of the burnt tenements not re-edified againe'*, included the guildhall. A plan was produced for a new guild house which seems to have been built by 1627. However it was not used as the town guildhall but let on a rental. Rook House could be that house.

There is a plan dating to the 1760s-80s (on page 55) showing a property *'supposed Town Lands called guild yard'* opposite the house. In Wymondham a guild yard could be on the opposite side of the road to the house to which it belongs. A terrier in the Town Book 1673-71 lists John Crowe occupying the yard with part of the house. In 1768 his daughter Mary Canham had it and the property belonged to the township.

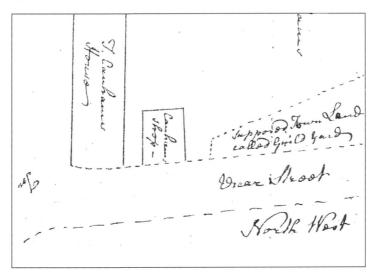

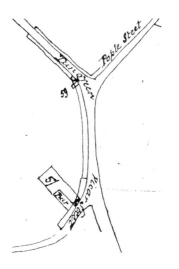

A plan of 1719, shows the lands in Wymondham called the Town Lands held for the benefit of a guild called St Peters, with number 57 as a tenement and garden in the same position as Rook House.

Mr & Mrs Bunn purchased Rook House in 1963 and Neal H Williams, author of the 'Oldest Law Firm in Norfolk', wrote this for them about its origins.

'The Charity School at Wymondham 1716-c 1816

There are records for the Wymondham Charity School for 30 boys. In the records of the Wymondham Town Lands Charity, there is a note of a house called the Towne House. This was let to John Bennett for the charity school for a rent of £6 pa from 1718. A notebook relating to Hendry's charity shows that a charity school was operating for most of the 18th century.'

'The evidence for this house lies in the Town Lands Charity where a map shows the transfer of two houses to **Cornelius Tipple** in exchange for the property in Middleton Street, known as the Priory, which became the grammar school and where Tipple was living .It could be from the position on the map (number 4), that Rook House is the one. The other house was Churchgate House (number 2), in Church Street.'

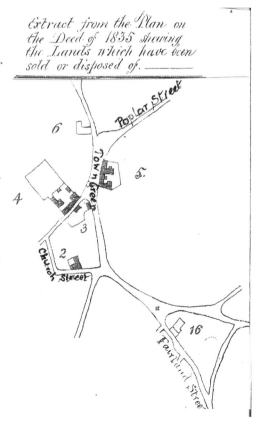

Tenants of Rook House

1680   Robert King, schoolmaster
1712   Mr Maidstone
1718   Master of the charity school
1733   Edward Durrant, linen weaver
1789   Edward Rudland, cooper
c.1825 Cornelius Tipple

'I am certain that it was the Guildhall and was among the buildings and land handed to the feoffes (trustees) *for the grammar school by Elizabeth I in 1559. I hope to sort it out one day as it is obviously one of the most important historical buildings in Wymondham.'*

Cornelius Tipple and the Fairland Church

Tipple was a member of a family of bombazine weavers. He went bankrupt and later left Wymondham for Salford in1853. He was Superintendent of the Fairland Church Sunday School and a deacon of the church. He kept detailed records of the church and when he left he was given a silver inkstand and a gold pen which cost 14 guineas.

Cornelius' Tipple's business card was found behind the mantelpiece in Rook House.

The Coronation of Queen Victoria 1838 and Rook House

A large number of children met at the Fairland Church and walked via Damgate to Lady's Lane then stopped outside Cavick House, the home of Mr W R Cann. They sang the

National Anthem and a coronation hymn specially composed by Mrs E Proctor. They continued two by two past the Abbey, along Vicar Street halting outside Rook House, the home of Cornelius Tipple. Here they sang hymns specially composed for the occasion, before they returned to the church for tea.

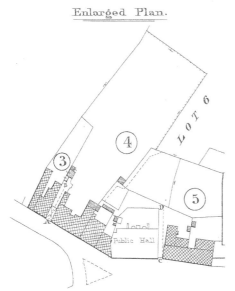

Enlarged Plan.

Rook House passed to Mrs Julia de Roubigne Beevor Clarke and was sold as part of her estate in 1894. The house is number 4 on this plan.

It was bought by Mrs Julia Frances Utten Brown (later Mrs Lilly). Her daughter married Captain Cautley of Abbotsford and she inherited the house in 1913. It was eventually sold to Mr & Mrs Bunn in 1963.

Rook House becomes a school again !

Rook House became a school once more, between 1922 and 1937. In 1912 Anna Smith had taken over a small private school in Town Green called Colwyn and she moved this to Rook House in 1922. The following is an extract from an appreciation in the local press of Anna's work on the occasion of her death in 1967 by a former pupil. J B A. from near Diss. It shows what she was like and what people thought of her.

' *"Guide Anna" as she was called, loved children. In fact she loved everyone and gave herself fully to her school. As a small boy of five, I was given her gentle but firm recipe for learning which included her 'miles of pennies' given to us on occasions for sweets and our lunchtime walks with a rest in the Abbey Church with a look at the coloured pictures.*

Colwyn School group, with Anna in the centre, 1931

'When the snow came she would drag out the massive sledge from the coalhouse and pull it herself with the older children up and down the street, forgetting lessons for the rest of the day.

There are few good things mentioned today and so few simple pleasures remembered, but Anna Smith gave sunshine and pleasures to many people, young and old during her long life.'

'Guide Anna' started the 1st Wymondham Guides in 1924 and in 1985, Dolly Attewell, herself a captain of the 2nd Wymondham Guides for 44 years, paid this tribute to her:

'In the 75th year of Guiding, 1985, we wanted a little project for her. There'll never be another Anna ! She had been buried 18 years but everybody looked up to her and still called her Captain. £284 was raised by the Trefoil Gild to buy a wheelchair for use in Wymondham Abbey in tribute to her.'

Mr & Mrs Bunn, new owners of Rook House

Mr & Mrs Bunn bought Rook House in 1963. The Bunns were themselves members of the long line of Wymondham characters who lived in this house.

During the Second World War Joan Bunn was a leading firewomen at the Hethersett HQ of the Fire Brigade. She was also a devoted member of the Royal British Legion and many other voluntary organisations. Ronald Bunn was the manager of the CWS Brush Company.

Mrs Bunn always thought that Rook House was the Guildhall and used to say that Mr Gledhill, solicitor who lived at number 14-16, Vicar Street, told her that the guild banners used to be kept in the cottage in the garden !

Number 10 Vicar Street, Conon House

This house was built at the end of the 16th century and is a high quality building. It has a timber frame but the base of the north brick wall dates from c. 1600 and is under the carriage arch of Rook House (number 8). The archway has been cut through the timber frame of Rook House and butted against the wall of Conon House. Its face was originally jettied and under built with brick.

A record of occupiers shows Edward Durrant, linen weaver, as living here in 1747. He also occupied Rook House in 1733. He died in 1789. During the 18th century the house was extended and it was altered in the 20th century.

Conon House, Abbotsford (number 12) and numbers 14-16, were all connected through the solicitors' Pomeroy & Son, which can be traced back to the mid 18th century and beyond.

Jeremiah Burroughs began the solicitor's business and was also a large landowner with brewing interests. He owned three inns, one of which was the White Swan, now Conon House. The early solicitor's offices were in Market Street, but by 1804, the office seems to have been a room in the White Swan. By 1818 Edward Clarke and John Mitchell were the partners and their office was also there. After Clarke's marriage in 1847, the office was moved to the Vicar Street house (number 12) now Abbotsford. Edward Clarke bought the White Swan as an inn in 1870 and in 1873 when he died, his widow surrendered the licence. When his widow died it was sold in 1894 to Mrs Utten Brown for £505.

In 1800 it was the last licensed house in Vicar Street.

Vicar Street c. 1900 – Abbotsford is located behind the trees on the left

Number 12, Abbotsford

In 1810 John Mitchell, solicitor, was paying tax as the owner – occupier of the Vicar Street House, now called Abbotsford.

In 1818 Edward Palmer Clarke became his partner. Their office was in the 'White Swan'. In 1847 Edward Palmer Clarke married Julia de Roubigne Beevor Fulcher. The solicitor's office was moved to the Vicar Street House soon after. An extension was built with a safe big enough for a man to stand in, a water closet and a 'bird room' to house the stuffed birds Julia inherited from Great Melton Hall and which she gave to Norwich Museum in 1873.

John Mitchell   E Palmer Clarke

In 1859 Edward Clarke bought it and lived there until his death in 1872. In 1879 the solicitor's office moved to 16, Vicar Street where an extension was built (number14). Julia had the Vicar Street House to herself. In an 1888 Directory, it was still called Vicar Street House.

After Julia died in 1894 the house was sold to Julia Frances Utten Brown. In 1913 Dorothea Julia her daughter, inherited it. She was married to Captain Harry Llewellyn Cautley. In the 1912 Kelly's Directory it was called Abbotsford.

Abbotsford as a Red Cross Hospital, 1914-18

Because of large numbers of casualties in the First World War, special Red Cross hospitals run by Voluntary Aid Detachment nurses, were set up all over the country. In November 1914, the Vicarage room in Church Street was opened with 12 beds. The vicar's wife Mrs Martin-Jones was the commandant. When more beds were required Captain & Mrs Cautley offered part of the house and grounds of Abbotsford. There were 20 beds in a large and small ward, a veranda with ten beds, bath and day room and the use of the lawn for bowls and cricket etc.

Abbotsford House

Mrs Martin-Jones was assisted by the ladies of Wymondham who held Red Cross certificates, with others helping with cooking. Dr Penn Young was the medical officer. Over 800 patients were treated and £951 was raised locally for the hospital which cost £6,000 for the four years of the war including government grants.

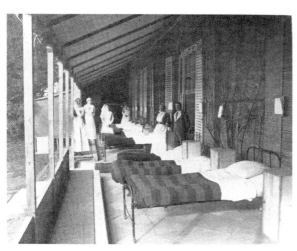

Two of the nurses, Vita Cross and Ella Wharton, kept autograph books in which the patients and staff wrote messages and drew pictures.

The veranda in the Abbotsford hospital

Abbotsford Hospital, staff and patients

Ella is your name,
Single is your Station,
Happy is the lucky man,
Who'll make the alteration,
When far away my dear you're carried,
And to some nice fellow married,
Remember me for friendships sake,
And send me a piece of wedding cake.

Cpt. W.T. Saville Auatero
32nd Royal Fusiliers
Wounded Aug 5. 191-

A soldier's tribute to Nurse Ella Wharton

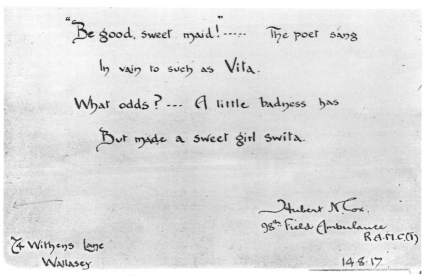

"Be good, sweet maid!..... The poet sang

In vain to such as Vita.

What odds? --- A little badness has

But made a sweet girl swita.

Hubert N Cox.
98th Field Ambulance
R.A.M.C.(T)

74 Withens Lane
Wallasey

14·8·17

A soldier's tribute to Nurse Vita Cross

Two examples of drawings by wounded soldiers

"Some "Girl for "Somme" Hero
A. Gallan 8th Royal Fusiliers
AUG 25th 16 Wounded at Ovillers (Somme)

By "Jock" 26·9·17

Between 1927-31 there was the Vicar Street Bowls Club which probably used the facilities at Abbotsford.

Numbers 14-16 Vicar Street

Rev William Papillon, the builder of the property
This property was built by Papillon, Vicar of Wymondham 1788-1836. He married Sarah Martha Drake of Cavick House in 1788 and lived there. After 12 years of marriage his wife died and he inherited a life interest in Cavick House.

Before he married, William had considered building himself a house opposite the vicarage and had bought ten acres of land. The house was built 1814-16. It had large reception rooms with servant's quarters in the basement with modern facilities. In 1817 he spent £68.8s 9d (£6,800) on a kitchen range and smoke jack. He sold his life interest in Cavick House which eventually went to W R Cann in 1826. He died at home in Vicar Street in 1836.

Some of Papillon's contributions to the life of the town

Papillon made significant contributions to Wymondham's story. Firstly, he promoted education for the children of the poor of the parish through working with the National Society of the Church of England and built a school in Church Street in 1812 (opposite the Abbey car park). This catered for some 200 children; he also helped to set up an infant's school in Lady's Lane, contributing to the wages of the teachers himself. In addition a Sunday school was started.

Secondly, he played a key role in re-routing the King's highway away from the Abbey and along the present route of Becketswell Road. Before 1827, the road went from Vicar Street through the churchyard to the porch. Papillon persuaded the public, landowners and the Crown of the benefits of the scheme. The resulting diversion took the road direct from Vicar Street to the Becketswell Bridge. Later he built a new churchyard wall.

Thirdly, in 1833 he was responsible for the setting up of the Papillon Trust in which some 20 acres of abbey meadow, owned by Papillon, between Damgate, and the churchyard, were transferred to the trust. This ensured that a beautiful and peaceful piece of land in the shadow of the former monastery was preserved for posterity.

An early print indicating how close the original highway passed to the church tower

After the vicar, a solicitor moves in to numbers 14-16

After Papillon's death his house in Vicar Street was bought by John Mitchell. By 1872, both Mitchell and Clarke the solicitors, had died. Some years later, number 16 became available and Edward Pomeroy a junior partner in the law firm, moved with his family from Abbotsford to number 16. In 1880 an extension to 16 was built for offices and was known as number 14.

Vicar Street showing no. 14, near left and the
Vicarage gate opposite

Edward Boyce Pomeroy, solicitor 1828--1902

Pomeroy lived at number 16 with his four daughters and two sons. A feature of the office was the shed at the back where parchment was prepared. Sheep skins were mainly used and were scraped and prepared for seizing.

Only two of his daughters married, one to Dr Lowe and one to Mr Fryer of Browick Hall.

John Bartle Pomeroy 1868-1952

Edward's second son's business was reduced during the First World War and he enjoyed sporting activities. He looked after the rainfall statistics for Wymondham every day.

Mrs Fisher was the cook for Mr John and Miss Bessie Pomeroy. She remembers those times in these words:

'The kitchen was in the basement and frogs would fall through the grating into it. Mr John would come down to the kitchen for a cup of tea. One day he said if ever there was a fire, I should save the glasses with the twisted stems in the drawing room cupboard as they were very valuable. He loved shooting and one day brought in a particularly maggoty pheasant and I had to strain the gravy! In 1953 after he died the house contents were auctioned and a large collection of glassware sold.'

In 1958 Mr Gledhill purchased the ownership of the business. He handled much of the Kimberley Hall estate sale.

In 1970 David Pennell became a partner. Mr Gledhill bought some old stables and garages opposite and converted them into offices. In 1983 they needed more accommodation so moved to Church Street.

The Vicarage

During the great fire of 1615 the vicarage was burnt and the vicar lost his clothes, books and other possessions. It was rebuilt and when William Papillon moved in, it looked much like it does today. But he was used to something grander with more land. After his marriage he lived at Cavick House but later moved to his new house, number 16. However he still wished to improve the vicarage. He wanted to build a new vicarage in the abbey grounds adjoining the old monastic tower. He built the abbey lodge in Church Street (opposite the Abbey Hotel), to serve as a lodge to his planned new vicarage.

However he could not proceed as a new vicarage could only be built on benefice land whereas this was his own. So instead he extended the vicarage garden and built a coach house and stable in 1833.

The Vicarage gateway

This drawing of the gateway was done in 1910 by the artist Colman Green, an admirer of Robert Kett. He wrote *'Kett's gateway was taken from Kett's house which was demolished about 1700. The arch stones and nail heads only are orignal'*.

We know that Kett had a property in Cavick. Mr Pomeroy, the solicitor who lived opposite the archway wrote, *'It is believed that Kett was tenant of the house formerly of William d'Albini, (founder of the Abbey) granted by him to the monastery in which the monks lived whilst the monastery was being built and which was opposite Cavick House.'*

So it is possible that the stone arch in the Vicarage gateway, shown in Colman Greens's drawing, came from this house.

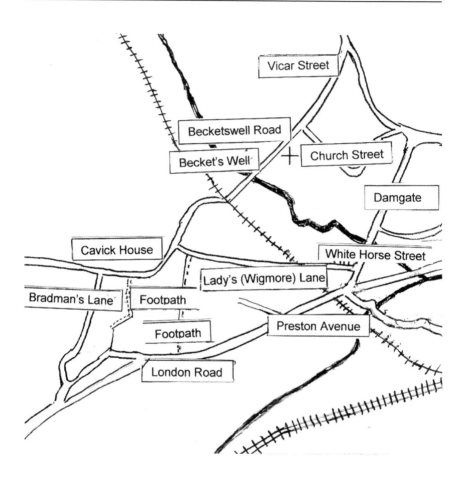

Church Street

In early times it was known as Churchgate, the street which was the gateway from Market Street to the Abbey Church.

Chamberlain's Lane

Originally this ran between Churchgate and Vicar Street near to the Vicarage Room, the predecessor of the present Abbey Hall. A remnant remains behind the Abbey Hall. The name maybe connected with the Abbey Chamberlain. One, James Blome, entertained women from the town according to the Bishops's Visitation report on the monastery in 1514.

The Vicarage Room

Known as the 'Tin Tabernacle' by locals because of its corrugated iron features, it was a meeting place for various social groups such as the Abbey Youth Club, dances, plays, socials and whist drives.

During World War One it was used as a Red Cross Voluntary Aid Detachment hospital, associated with the one in Abbotsford, Vicar Street.

Prior to and during World War Two it was used by Civil Defence groups like the ARP for training purposes and the military. Another wartime use was as a meeting place for evacuee mothers run by the WVS.

After the war it was used for social events, like this birthday party in the 1960s, showing the Earl of Kimberley with his wife on the right.

The Vicarage Room was eventually demolished. The present **Abbey Hall** was built and officially opened in May 1970.

12, Church Street

After a big demonstration on the Fairland in 1919, Edwin Gooch a journalist and founding father of the local Labour Party, established an administrative base at this property. The Labour Institute was opened here by Lord Kimberley in 1920. Later in the year Gooch, George Edwards' political agent, stood outside the door of this house to celebrate a famous by-election victory for Labour in south Norfolk.

Lord Kimberley, centre with George Edwards on left and Edwin Gooch on right, outside the Labour Institute in 1920.

Labour supporters outside committee rooms at 12, Church Street.

Edwin Gooch seated 5th left, Ethel Gooch 7th left

The Abbey Hotel

The site which was used to build the hotel was originally occupied by a barn and cottages. These were demolished about 1888, after which Semmence built the Red House. This in due course became the Abbey Hotel.

The Red House was owned by Mr Newton of Newton, Pollock & Wilson who had offices in Fairland Street, currently the

Handbag and Leather Shop. Between 1893 and 1904, the top bedroom of the house was used as a Roman Catholic chapel.

Dudley Bowles, a popular hotelier 1948-86
Dudley from Kimberley, came to the Abbey Hotel in 1948. He had run a hotel in King's Lynn. Mrs Phyllis Little another director, was head cook and worked there for 36 years. During the Bowles era, the Abbey hotel became a very popular venue for visitors and locals alike. We first tasted pheasant in the restaurant, but the jugged hare was a step too far !

The Abbey Hotel in its heyday.

The tariff
5 to 6 guineas a week
1 guinea to 25/- a day
Room & breakfast, 15/- to 25/-
Lunch, 4/-
Tea, 2/-
Dinner, From 5/-
Dogs, 1/6d a day

No alcohol allowed

There was a gentlemen's agreement between Mr Bowles and Mr Fred Turnell at the Green Dragon nearby. The hotel provided the food for weddings and dinners but had no alcohol licence. The drinks came from the Green Dragon, which did not even sell crisps or nuts.

8, Church Street - Churchgate House

This property has late medieval origins with additions in the 16th century. In 1672 Robert Dey bequeathed it for the use of the Grammar School. A number of boarders resided there.

The Green Dragon

Next door is the **Green Dragon** which dates from the 15th century. It has an interesting carved head of a bearded man supporting its jetty. The front windows are believed to have been formerly shop windows. Robert Kett's brother William, had a butcher's business in the street and it is possible that he displayed his wares at one of these windows.

The Green Dragon in the 1930s. The petrol pump next door, belonged to the National Benzole chain.

Reggie Bird recalls his wartime memories

'I had the garage next to the Green Dragon – National Benzole. Soldiers at the searchlight at Cavick used to hire a car to go back to London on Friday night and come back Saturday.

My wife went in the Fire Brigade but did not stay long. I joined the volunteer Fire Brigade in 1936 and left as Chief Officer, Volunteer Brigade, to be an Area Transport officer for the National Fire Service. We used to practice at the lake at Kimberley Hall. I saw Lord Kimberley before he went off to London, where he was killed by enemy action that night.'

Tales about tunnels

There have always been stories of a tunnel from the Green Dragon's cellar which supposedly ran to the Abbey. However, drainage and road works have exposed old brick sewers that run under the main streets of the town. The tunnels were half round and about a metre high and 1.5m across; the floor was covered with running water and debris. This was at the southern end of Church Street where the water formerly disgorged into an open dyke, replaced by a pipe in former years, to the river. Going up the street towards the town, the tunnels became smaller and oval. It was these that occasionally gave rise to stories of 'secret tunnels' and the like.

Becket's Chapel – background to a special presentation to a special man

In 1926 George Edwards stepped down as the Labour candidate for South Norfolk. Edwin Gooch was adopted as the new Labour candidate in 1929. In 1931 he stood for Labour in 'a religious crusade' against the National Government of Macdonald and the Tories. Though defeated, he did increase the Labour vote. Edwards was honoured with a special certificate to mark his huge contribution to the Labour Party in Norfolk. In 1926, this was presented to him outside Becket's Chapel.

Gooch is seen inset, and holding the certificate, with Edwards on his right

1, Church Street - Proctor's shoe shop
Arthur Proctor moved into his Church Street shop in 1930. Part of this shop was formerly the Goat Inn which was sold by auction in 1928.

The Goat Inn is on the near left in this photo

In the Grisaugh Manor Court book of 1558, this building was described as one *'under which water runneth'*. Mr Proctor described a stone in the stable, now built over, and under which there was water. Thomas Martin the antiquarian, recorded the remains of a pipe in the corner of Damgate in 1722. It was part of the system which carried water from the spring Estapil, in the conduit field, near the roundabout on Browick Road which leads to the A11, for use in the monastery and recently mentioned by the late Paul Cattermole in his book 'Wymondham Abbey'.

Water ran in a lead pipe, possibly along the Lizard, where a former resident recalled an ancient stone under which soft water ran. It ran into the town centre and via Church Street to the monastery. Incidentally, at Langley Abbey near Loddon, the monks also piped water from a distant spring.

Another notable occupant of Church Street, was **George Reeve** who opened his printing business there before moving to other premises. Incidentally, George Reeve told Arthur Proctor that his business would fail as people walked on the other side of the street and would not cross. Proctor's shop survived until 2012 !

Charles Ayton, Quarry owner

The building now occupied by Greenland, Houchen & Pomeroy, solicitors, was the offices of Charles Ayton, quarry owner in 1925. After his death, his widow moved opposite The Green Dragon and ran a wine and spirit shop for money to bring up the children.

Opposite the Abbey Hotel

The cottages below were demolished to build the four houses opposite the Abbey Hotel c. 1888. Mr RV Reyner built the fifth detached one.

The Abbey Lodge

In 1828 the Rev Papillon had the house called the Abbey Lodge, built as a lodge for the new vicarage he wanted to build in the churchyard. It was made available to his housekeeper and her husband for their lifetime.

The Abbey churchyard wall

Stone from the monastery after the dissolution in 1538, was salvaged and can be seen incorporated into the churchyard wall as coping stones. Within the churchyard is the **school room**, formerly the school founded by Rev Papillon in 1812 to educate poor children in the town.

Becket's Chapel

Thomas Becket, Archbishop of Canterbury, was murdered at the altar of his own cathedral in December 1170. He was canonised in February 1173.

William d'Albini III founded this chapel dedicated to Becket and his own family c. 1174. About 1180 the chapel was described by d'Albini as '*standing in my market place of Wymondham surrounded by a hedge*'. **This** market place may have been under the jurisdiction of the prior while the one on the site of the present market, was run by Grisaugh Manor.

Becket became a popular saint in Wymondham and Becket's Chapel was well endowed, two monks being kept. The religious gild of St Thomas was founded there in 1187 and maintained lights before the altar.

In the 15th century the chapel was repaired and the late decorated style of c. 1400 replaced the earlier Norman architecture.

The abolition of the gilds

Although Henry VIII had abolished the gilds dedicated to St Thomas and taken their funds, parishioners continued to celebrate Becket's appointment as Archbishop of Canterbury. In July 1549 on the eve of the annual fair to celebrate this, it has been suggested that the old church mystery plays were performed in the chapel and that plays performed on carts and a pageant processed through the town.

In the list of possessions drawn up in Edward VI's reign (1547-53), are the costumes for the '*game playe*' but whether these belonged to the parish gilds or the Watch & Play Society is unclear. The latter enjoyed acting and there are records of payments made for '*a canvas to the gyant*' and for '*a payer of devils shoes.*'

The link with Robert Kett

Robert Kett had been active in trying to preserve Becket's Chapel for the town in 1538. He was a member of the gild of St Thomas and involved in the Watch and Play Society. In 1549 Kett showed great courage in standing up to the excessive power of the Norfolk gentry and ultimately the Tudor state. A plaque commemorating the events that began at the Wymondham Fair in July 1549, is by the door to Becket's Chapel.

In 1545 Henry VIII had decreed that all religious gilds attached to Wymondham parish church should close. This was confirmed in 1547 in Edward VI's reign, but it was said that proceeds from the sale of any properties left, should be used to establish schools for boys.

The chapel as a school

In 1549 more lands which had belonged to St Peter's and St Thomas's gilds were sold and some rented out. The profits were paid to the churchwardens. These lands became known as the '*Towne lands*'. The chapel was rented out but not initially as a school. In 1559, John Flowerdew, sole trustee of the land and tenements owned by St Thomas's gild, surrendered them to the Queen. In 1561 she granted them to key Wymondham inhabitants for use to pay a suitable schoolmaster and build and maintain a school in the town. In the same year Wymondham Free School was founded, later Wymondham Grammar school. The school was here until changes in 1835, when it moved to Priory House and other buildings in Middleton Street. After this, Becket's Chapel was little used for several decades.

Drawing by Thomas Jeckell 1871, showing various outbuildings attached to the chapel

By 1875 the chapel had been converted into a public hall and all the associated outbuildings were pulled down ie. the coal house, town stocks, a lock-up and the fire station.

Becket's Chapel, late 19th century, after the outbuildings had been demolished

The grammar school closed in 1903. In due course it was used for town and parish meetings until 1948 when it became the town library. Janet Smith was librarian for many years, a legend in the town, fund of local knowledge and source of many unusual tales, none more so than one about bees ! A colony of bees lived in the wall of the chapel but seemed to have perished in the severe winter of 1981. Later that year Janet noticed signs of activity and Ted Ellis the naturalist said a passing swarm may have been attracted by the smell of previous inhabitants ! Swarming bees have been known to halt traffic in Church Street but the help of a beekeeper, who worked at the Abbey Hotel, was called in to solve the problem.

After the opening of the new library in Back Lane in 2008, Becket's Chapel became the Arts Centre. It is still in the hands of the Wymondham Grammar School Trust.

Wymondham Abbey

The church before the Abbey

The parish of Wymondham, the second largest in Norfolk, is thought to have been an Anglo Saxon royal or aristocratic estate which may have become an ecclesiastical unit. There may have been a 7th or 8th century Saxon church on the site which could have been a minster.

Wymondham Priory founded 1107

William d'Albini had come to England in 1090 hoping to acquire land. He became a loyal subject of William II. Soon after Henry I became king in 1100, he was appointed as pincerna, with the right to carry the royal cup at the coronation. He was granted the 'honour' of Buckenham which included the manor of Wymondham. His marriage to Maud Bigod in 1107 brought a large dowry.

He founded a priory in 1107 intending the building to be used by the prior and 12 monks and also by the townspeople as their parish church, a recipe for future strife between the monastery and the town. The monastic tower and the larger west tower built later by the townspeople, are symbols of that trouble.

The priory was a high status building, visible for miles, underlining William's power, wealth and prestige. In religious terms, the monks could offer prayers for the d'Albini family and provide social services to the locality.

The coming of the priory was a turning point in the history of Wymondham, which was gradually transformed from a Saxon centre into a busy and thriving Norman town.

Excavations

1833-34   The mummified bodies of d'Albini's auburn-haired wife and unborn child, were found in coffins near the high altar. Maud died in the 1120s.

1980   During the replacement of surface water sewers in the town, a trench was dug across the Abbey meadow north east from the weir to the angle of Church Street. A large number of sheep, pig, cow and horse bones together with others from geese, rabbit and hare and even the back legs of a fallow deer were found. This suggested the area may have been used for dumping waste from the monastic kitchens. Most of the pottery unearthed was 13th-15th century Grimston ware.

1992-93   Westfields, opposite the Abbey was excavated , and some evidence of a building of early date found. Samuel Woodward, who conducted the 1833 excavation had suggested the second site of the founder's mansion was in this area.

2002-03   This survey provided some evidence that the abbey was the **third** church on the site. The church on the site before the present building had sealed within its foundations, an earlier burial indicating an even earlier church in the vicinity. Foundation and wall fabric representing a late Saxon or early Norman church was also sealed within the nave arcade of the present church. Both artefacts and features found, indicate activity possibly dating to Roman times and there were numerous fragments of medieval glass and a medieval fish hook, More than 20 skeletons almost all pre-dating the present building were found, and at least one was early Saxon.

More information about the building of the monastery

The late Paul Cattermole's study of the Wymondham Register from the British Library, has revealed previously unknown detail about the monastery

Built of Caen and Barnack stone, some architectural features may have arrived 'ready made'. In the 12th century water levels on the Tiffey were higher than they are today – when the first bypass was created and the river course was altered it was 15 feet down before solid ground was reached. The stone may have come to Wymondham by barge along the Tiffey – the monastery kept a barge at Carleton Forehoe. Near the current Becketswell Bridge was a small community called Stanbrige, perhaps housing those working on the priory.

Some memories of the Abbey

Miss Mary Lowe, daughter of Dr Lowe

'It was very quiet then (c.1912) *and there was more poverty. The vicar and churchwardens, administered charitable gifts of vouchers to buy things. The old maids gift for spinsters of good character, was 2/6d. We had to be careful with money. I remember my father raising the chauffeur's wages to a £1 a week'.*

Jack Bowden - The Bowdens were involved in repairing the Abbey after World War One. Jack is refering to the reredos.

'A message came from the vicarage asking one of us to meet the architect Sir Ninian Comper with a 30 stave ladder, a mallet and a wood chisel. The architect was sitting in the nave looking at his work. One of the larger figures on the right hand side, St Andrew, had to have a piece chipped off so the figure could be moved half an inch. Everything had to be perfect. It's never been touched since the crucifix was re-hung onto the roof. It was supposed to be a memorial for Mrs Alice Martin-Jones, commandant of the Wymondham Red Cross hospital. There was

a subscription list of 1,000. Some of the parish did not agree with a memorial in the Abbey, feeling that all denominations should be represented on it. On a pillar is a panel describing what the reredos was for. Father painted it in Parson's paint.'

The Abbey's west tower used for an execution, 1549

The execution of William Kett, brother of Robert, for his part in the great rebellion of 1549, was described by Edward Pomeroy (d.1902), solicitor and antiquary, as follows:
'Robert Kett was hung in chains over Norwich castle and the stout hospitaller his brother William, after a dip in boiling pitch, was hung in his black robes over the architectural marvel he tried to preserve (the west tower of abbey church)......William Kett's body fell bone from bone only on the last day of Elizabeth's reign 25th March 1603.'

It is the stuff of legends – another account says that the skeleton was removed in 1578 on the orders of Elizabeth I when she was staying at Kimberley Hall.

Incidentally, a recent visitor to the museum said that you could still see the shadow of Kett's skeleton on the west tower !

The Great Restoration of the Abbey 1901-08
The key figures behind the restoration, were the Rev. Archibald Parker, vicar of Wymondham, 1898-1905, Mr E B Pomeroy, senior churchwarden and Mr RV Reyner, secretary to the restoration committee.
Mrs Willett daughter of a former vicar contributed £14,000 more than half the total cost of repairs The contractor was Rattee & Kett of Cambridge. The latter was a descendant of William Kett who was hanged from the west tower. Despite difficulties with raising money, the debt was cleared and the Rev. Parker returned to preach at the Thanksgiving.

A Victorian Vicar's family at the Abbey west door

Becketswell Road
Named after the spring known as Becket's Well whose water was believed by medieval pilgrims to have sacred and healing properties.

Westfields opposite the Abbey church, was the last house to be built of Wymondham brick for Mr George Marwood, the Technical Director at Briton Brush factory.

Childhood memories of the Tiffey
The river Tiffey was my playground all the year round. Many hours were spent mucking about in and along the river with my brothers and friends. Our house was opposite the Abbey so we could get to the river over the fields without going on to the road. In the 1930s and 40s there were no fears about being

molested or of violence. We would just tell our mum that we were going to the river to play and all she would say would be 'don't be late for lunch'. We would build dams, catch sticklebacks or other tiddlers and bring them home in jars. We would play pooh sticks at the bridge by Becket's Well. The well was a natural spring with deliciously refreshing water. We would see how far we could walk down the river before it got too deep. During the spring we would hunt for bird's nests. If we found one we would take one egg and blow it before we got home.

I've seen the river in spate with the water at the top of the bridge arches. The fields would be flooded and we would see how far we could get along the river until it got too deep. Sometimes we got as far as the railway bridge near Dereham Road. Usually we could walk under it - I remember it being a dark, muddy tunnel. In winter during frosty weather, flooded areas would freeze and we would slide and skate on them and play ice hockey.

Michael Marwood 2006, (son of George Marwood)

Becket's Well

In the garden of the last house on the right before Tiffey Bridge, is a spring whose water flows into the river. In the Middle Ages it was known as Becket's Well whose waters were believed by pilgrims, to have sacred and healing properties.

90

Robert Semmence's turnery

On the Abbey side of the river among trees, the cottage on the left, just before Becketswell Bridge, was the site of the wood turning factory of Robert Semmence & Son. Since medieval times Wymondham had been a centre for the craft of wood turning and was famous for its spoons. In 1907 the factory was destroyed by fire but the cottage was saved – by water from the Tiffey. Semmence, born 1815, started as a wood turner but in time was producing spoons, forks, hand cups and bowls from local timber. When demand for these declined he began to make brush backs, scythe handles and the like at his Cavick sawmills. One of his best customers for brush backs, was S D Page of Norwich.

In the photo below, the roof and upper windows of a property surrounded by trees and bushes are visible. It was a part of a property transfer by the Rev Papillon to nine trustees in 1833 – '*All that messuage or tenement.... Late in the several occupations of William Rudling and Henry Lovett'*.

The property has had many additions but the core of the house appears much older than 19th century. The school in Church Street and the Infants School in Lady's Lane were in the deal. The trustees could let the land but not the schools, and the income

91

must pay for the education in the two schools set up by the Rev. Papillon. The trustees were to start and continue evening service between 5 and 10pm. A lecturer would preach a sermon and be paid £40 a year.

In the 21st century the trustees still own the Church Street premises and have stewardship of the Abbey meadows.

The Railway level crossing in Cavick
This crossing was on the line to Dereham and the north Norfolk coast with connections at Wymondham to the main London to Norwich line. Bells would indicate the approach of a goods or passenger train. Under the crossing keeper's cottage there was a culvert and the outside toilet was a double seater. Water came from Becket's Well which was still believed to be a recipe for long life !

The level crossing in the early 1900s

The crossing keeper waiting for a train at the Cavick level crossing, c. 1960s
The line to Dereham and beyond was opened to passengers in 1847 and closed in 1969.
The Mid Norfolk Railway to Dereham from the Abbey halt station, opened in May 1999.

Cavick and Lady's Lane

The name of the lane may be linked to the convent of St Mary or 'Our Lady.'

There are many questions about the story of Cavick and the area of Lady's Lane, formerly called Wigmore Lane or Wigmor Walles. In 1577 it was referred to as *'the common lane by the walls of the scite of the late abbie of Wymondham called Wigmor Walles.'*

The road from Thetford came in roughly parallel to Bradman's Lane along a route called Greengate. It crossed the Tiffey near Becketswell Bridge, ran close to the southern boundary of the churchyard and emerged into an open market place.

About 1120 d'Albini changed the course of the King's Highway to insulate the monastery from travellers and other activities and *'turned the king's highway by his house, which had formerly been against the church'*. The Thetford road may have been diverted along the present line of Lady's (Wigmore) Lane, with a sharp bend near d'Albini's new manor house. It joined the Buckenham Road to cross Dam Bridge and entered the town that way. The significance of Wigmore Lane in the road system is shown by an act of Geo. II 1746, *'to repair the highway from Wymondham to Attelborough and Wymondham to Hethersett and from the mouth of Wigmore Lane to Walkgate, Attleborough'*.

William d'Albini's new manor house
The late Paul Cattermole believed that this could have been on the site of the present Cavick House or possibly on the opposite side of the road to it. Solicitor and antiquarian, E B Pomeroy had his own ideas:
>*'It is believed that Kett was the tenant of the house formerly of Wm. d'Albini..... granted by him to the monastery*

93

in which the monks lived whilst the monastery was building and which was opposite Cavick House, and that he was on the best terms with his landlords the monks.'

When we first came to Wymondham it was suggested that the site on the corner of Lady's Lane, opposite Cavick House, had been the location of Kett's house. In a list of Kett's possessions at his trial, was a property described as being :

'In the street called Cakwyke (Cavick*) in Wymondham between the close of the late abbot and convent of St Mary in Wymondham called Wygmore on the south, and the King's Highway on the north…'*

Cavick House

The rear of Cavick House, 1892

This wonderfully restored property is on a site which could have been occupied since the 12th century. The original core of the present house dates from c. 1650 and was extended by weaver John Drake c. 1720. Richard and Sarah Drake then inherited the 500 acre Cavick estate. Sarah died in 1793 and Richard in 1802. The Rev. William and Sarah Martha Papillon then became owners of the house. Local brewer William Cann bought it in 1825.

94

The 457th
Searchlight
Battalion of the
69th Searchlight
Regiment, in
1940, were
located in
Cavick

Tannery and meadows
In 1788 Richard Drake of Cavick House sold a property called Tan Vatt meadows *'next to the Abbey lands on the east, a certain lane called Wigmore Lane on the south and next the King's Highway as well north as west ....being the possessions of the late dissolved Abbey of Wymondham.'*
Robert Kett was a tanner as well as a landowner, so these meadows may have a connection with Kett.

Some memories of Lady's Lane
In the 20th century others remember a building in Lady's Lane. Dick Hewitt said, *'there was a big old church arch in the lane. The Rev Jones bought it and dismantled it stone by stone marking each one'*
An anonymous writer described Lady's Lane thus: *'the overgrown rodent infested bank along the lane.... actually part of the Abbey* (boundary wall*) wall and also the site near the end of the lane where, till some months ago stood an arch which was an entrance to the Abbey gardens and which has been removed for no good reason'*.
A decorated stone was also recorded as found in Lady's Lane.

Further along the lane towards Damgate, the Rev. Papillon also set up an Infants school described in a deed as, *'all that cottage... now or late in the occupation of John Poll together with the rooms adjoining thereunto now used for an infant school'*.

Papillon's Infant school could be one of the two buildings arrowed on this photo of Briton Brush factory site, next to Lady's Lane going left towards Damgate. The former White Horse public house can be seen in the background.

The Briton Brush factory

Modern brush making began in Wymondham in 1886 when **S D Page & Sons** of Norwich, an important brush making company, started a small brush works in Lady's Lane where land was inexpensive. Another attraction of the area was a good labour force, plentiful woodlands and a strong local tradition of craftsmanship.

There was also a sawmill and a turnery to supply stocks and handles to the Norwich and Wymondham factories, making the Lady's Lane outfit a key element in Page's business.

Within a decade there were 200 workers here and over 20 of the recently invented Gane brush filling machines were in use.

The brush filling room – working on the Gane machines, 1901

Within the next few years there were 30,000 poles for stocks and 750,000 brush backs in the drying sheds in the Wymondham factory.

In 1920 S D Page and **D Matthew & Son** a London brush maker, merged to form the biggest brush making business in the British Empire. It was named the **Briton Brush Company** and became a landmark in brush making and Wymondham history. By the mid 1930s nearly all the manufacturing was carried out at Wymondham. A railway siding had been built in 1916 linking the factory to the main line, facilitating both the import of raw materials such as bristles from China and the export of finished products throughout the world.

Briton Brush railway linked the main line. The pole yards and the Abbey can be seen in the background.

Despite difficulties after the First World War and the Great Depression, Briton steadily expanded in the 1930s. Brush making

97

materials were imported from Asia, Africa and South America, particularly the bristle of wild boar, though most of the timber came from the locality. It was said that two fully grown beech trees were consumed every day ! A company slogan was *'Briton Brush sweeps the world'*, another, *'a brush for every use'*. The range and speed of production was remarkable. Over 2,000 different brushes were being made and some 30,000 brushes produced daily. At its peak some 800 people were employed at the Lady's Lane factory, making it the biggest employer in the town. The company was also blessed with innovative engineers. New machinery was designed in its workshops and a turbo generator was introduced to utilize waste wood to provide electric power. The weir on the Tiffey, created a pool of water which was pumped to the factory to cool the condenser of the steam turbine. Briton Brush became a world leader in its field because of skilful engineers, designers, and craftsman and a hardworking and loyal workforce who were well treated by the owners.

Some workers were bussed in from villages, and cottages were built to let to others near the factory. There were excellent amenities at the factory with social and sporting clubs, a concert band, works' outings and even a Christmas bonus. Briton Brush was a great supporter of families, many of whom had two or even three generations working there.

At work in the factory during the 1950s.

At play !
All aboard the Briton
Brush
Express for a works
outing

Eventually, decline set in because of cheap foreign competition and the coming of plastic which replaced many household goods. But for over half a century Briton Brush made an indelible impact on the economic and social life of the town. It put Wymondham on the industrial map and helped to improve the lives of many families.

In 1968 the company merged with Chadwick Hollins to become Briton Chadwick Ltd and in 1982 the Wymondham factory was taken over by the newly formed Windmill Brush Company. In 1985 Briton Brush ceased to trade as an independent unit.

Memories of Briton Brush

John Fulcher
'At Briton I worked from 8am -7pm (55hrs a week) and had 5s/5d a week in the warehouse. We had a week's holiday but did not get paid during stock taking. I was there 50 years. I was working 14-15 hrs more than I had been but I liked it. There was not enough money at the solicitor's office – only 5s.'

Dick Hewitt

'*I went to the Briton. The sawmill there was driven by overhead shafting and a big pulley wheel. There were no guards and there were a lot of accidents. We made a guard with wood and wire netting. One side was hinged to open. When the lady inspector came she missed nothing and we had to guard everything.*

In the war (1939-45) we bought a big roll of blackout and had to cover all the skylights. We had a ring and ropes at each end to close them. My wife and some of the other women made them. We had to draw them at a certain time in the afternoon and check that no light was showing. Then we put wire netting underneath in case blast shattered the glass. I did a lot of painting of the whole factory using Indestructible paint and used a reddish brown with yellow window frames, then cream and green and then blue. My sister Joyce worked there on a sanding wheel – the worst job was in the machine room where there was terrible dust. They took the iron off the roof which was replaced with asbestos sheets. It was very cold in there in 1963-4 with six weeks of solid frost and snow'.

Dolly Attewell

'*When I left school I went to work for the Rev Jackson and then Briton Brush for 28 years. I worked on the machines and I got picked by Mrs Page to work on them. The machines were all daylong making scrubbing brushes. My father Jimmy was a night watchman there for six years at one time. The machines were never that successful. Too quick. You had to keep oiling the parts.*

I had a lovely time – there was a lot of machinery and noise. You had to be able to speak up for yourself. I went on to making toy sweeping brushes. I did not seem to get on the bonus scheme. I was working hard and I never lost a minute. One day I went up to the office and asked for Mr Matthew. He said, 'what's the matter' and I said I felt very unhappy about not getting any bonus. I got a bonus after that! We had concert parties and I organised a hockey team. We had our bad days its true, but we really had a marvellous time. I made clothes, nail, scrubbing and lavatory brushes. I also did packing and trimming - most of the things in the factory. I liked being with engineers.'

London Road

Until Preston Avenue was completed between 1929 and 1934, the town did not extend beyond Ivygreen Farm and the London Tavern towards Attleborough.

Bowden Terrace

This terrace had been built in the 1890s by the Bowden brothers. There used to be an old pump for water and soak away drains for the residents.

Many old Wymondham families lived here – the Yaxleys, Lynchs, Wilson, an insurance agent, Mr Bunn the postman, Blyth, Royle and Mr Brummage, a cabinet maker who was in the Fire Brigade and the band. He lived to 99 years of age.

Leslie Kerridge has this story to tell about Ivygreen Farm:

'My dad lived at the shop (the butchers'*) in Market Street (*now Motor Accessories*), but also owned Ivygreen Farm on the London Road opposite Preston Avenue. My father kept cows where the fire station is now. The garage, (*now Toucan Hire*), was built in 1928 when motoring was taking off.'*

Preston Avenue

According to Leslie Kerridge this road was named after a Dr Preston. When the council began to build homes at Preston Avenue, some were set aside for Briton Brush employees. During the period 1929-34, 48 houses were completed.

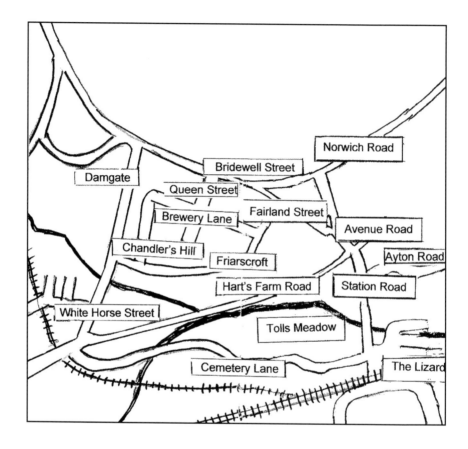

White Horse Street

Which came first, the street name or the White Horse public house ?

An early photo of White Horse Street – the White Horse public house is in the far left background

Landowner Thomas Randall left this house, one of several on his estate to his grandsons in 1738. Soon after it became the White Horse, seen here in the early 1900s.

Memories of George Duffield b. 1889

The **Duffield** family had a blacksmith's business near Damgate Bridge on the right hand side going out of the town. The memories of **George Duffield** shed much light on family and working life in the street.

'We had a smithy in Whitehorse Street. They used to call it Damgate in those days. Father's letters and post used to be marked Damgate Bridge House. Now it's Whitehorse St. I don't remember that name in those days.'

Duffield – much more than a blacksmith

The Duffields at work

'My trade was engineering and I went in with my father. He did everything – grass cutters, farm implements, shoeing, woodwork side, tumbrels and wagons repaired and painted. We had an engineering shop at the back of the shoeing place, where there was a drilling and screwing machine. We had a Lister engine and a shaft was up here that drove the machines. When we put new tyres on cart wheels there were all the holes to drill. He would not start the engine up for one – had to do half a dozen. You heat the rim and put the tyre on – it shrinks on but you have to put the rivets in. Two men worked for my father. He did the engineering side and the others

104

did shoeing and blacksmith's side. They worked 6am – 6pm, lunch 1-2pm, breakfast 830-9, made by mother.'

Jobs for a boy

'When I was 8 or 9, I had work to do. There was a yard in front of the house which had to be swept on Saturday. There was kindling to be chopped for fires. Saturday was cleaning day for the living room and kitchen. We had bread and cheese or bread and dripping Wednesdays & Saturdays. Cooking day was Friday – the oven was in the wall. Gas came in the later part of my schooldays.

*The fireplace had a heater stove with a hob each side. On the hob was a big cauldron always full of water and one and half gallon iron kettle. We used a ewer to get water (*from a well by the Tiffey), *a cauldron for washing water and drinking water was in a kettle.*

Outside the back kitchen was a big tank – 1000 galls of water – all water from the building drained into there and there was a tap through into the kitchen. You can see the path down to the well (by Damgate Bridge) *before the sewer came. I had to go across with father who made a hoop with two pails and I went across every morning and when I got home at night and fetched two more. There was an old tin bath under kitchen table and I poured water in there for cooking.'*

105

Being a good neighbour

'At the back of the house was the engineering shop and a toilet in the yard. Behind that the laundry – a copper and 6ft tub they used to salt pigs in. Father killed two pigs for bacon and ham. Our next door neighbours the Butchers were very poor and had a fish and chip shop. Mother gave them the liver and lights. The legs were used to make pork cheese and 4 hams. Heads were cooked and given away. Sides of pigs were put in tub and rubbed with salt and hams too. He used to put them on the barrow and take to Halls butchers to smoke them in old muslin curtains. Our big garden, went down to Briton fields where they're now building.

When I was a youngster you could walk straight onto the meadow – there was no Briton factory there. They started to bring timber in for the pole yards.

*I did not want to do horse shoeing 6am-7pm. and so I became one of three regulars who worked at **Wicklewood Workhouse**. I looked after boilers and carted the coal from the cellar – one was a schoolmaster and another a gentleman's servant old Jim. Mr Mustoe was master and his wife was matron.*

Mr Horne looked after people who came in at night; they were fed and put to bed. They had to do so much work before they went in the morning – gardening, coal hauling etc. Water had had to be pumped from the well for the boiler. Everything was steam cooked.'

Friarscroft Lane

The origin of the name has been subject to some debate. The word 'croft' means a piece of land. On the Enclosure town map of 1810, what we know as Friarscroft is unnamed, but Brewery Lane is called Friars's Lane. On his map of Wymondham at the time of the Fire (1615), John Wilson marks the area of the modern Chandler's Hill development, as Friarscroft.

In the deeds of no. 43 Damgate, which has some land behind it on Chandler's Hill, the adjoining property is described as abutting upon *'the lands of the fee of the Brethren of Choseley towards the east,'* and on another occasion, *'the croft of the Brethren of Choselies'* is mentioned.

W. d'Albini gave the manor of Choseley to the church of St Lazarus of Jerusalem at Burton and the *'Brethren'* there. Coincidentally, there were two brethren and a master to collect alms from those who passed Westwade Chapel on Chapel Bridge. It is possible therefore, that Friarscroft gets its name from the links with *'the Brothers of Choseley'*.

Friarscroft, looking towards the
Sun Inn - early 1900s

George Duffield recalls looking up Friarscroft with the Sun Inn on the right and on the other side the home of Mr Harvey, the bellman or town crier (seen here). *'He dressed up to read the news of coming events in Wymondham.'* Ian Slaughter was born in the small cottage behind the Sun and could look straight into the bar from his small window.

In the late 1790s or early 1800s Providence Chapel was opened in Friarscroft by the Baptist Church. It was capable of holding 200 people.

In 1897 a cottage and stable were obtained at the top of the new road leading from the Market Place (Queen Street), for a new chapel. The Friarscroft premises – a meeting house, yard or burial ground and dwelling house and garden were eventually sold to Henry Moore a blacksmith. This is now a private house.

Chandler's Hill

The chandler (candle maker), was a key figure in medieval times when candles were the main source of light so vital to all households. The proximity of the parish church and monastery both consuming large numbers of candles, provided a ready local market. It is possible that a number of chandlers lived in this area giving the road its name.

However in later times there were tenter frames in a tenter yard in the area. Woollen cloth was attached to tenter hooks to stretch it. In 1851, 18 people were working as weavers in this road.

Looking up Chandler's Hill from Friarscroft

Tubby Fulcher, b. 1906, of Queen Street

'Where the Chandler's Hill housing development is now, was once a large vegetable garden and orchard owned by the Cranness family who lived in Victoria Villa. His father lived in Yarmouth or Lowestoft. At one time the yard was full of timbers from a ship or something – he could have bought wrecks.
The Cranness family built the houses in Queen Street. Mr Cranness was rich and owned much property in the town including Tolls Meadow and lived off the rents. ***Chandler's Close*** *was his garden where he grew crops to sell.* He was *a gentleman's gentleman'.*

George Duffield recalled that *'Up the lane on the left* (Friarscroft), *was a small sweet shop run by Mrs Hunt. You come to a large house on the left, now an old people's home – Pennybrick Hall. Mr Daniels whose son had the greenhouses at Northfield, lived there.*

Just past that on the left side was a garage that was a weaving factory run by Mr Poll (see photo*) who lived on the Lizard. A short thickset man, he gave my father quite a lot of work sharpening sheep shears. It was Hovells horsehair weaving factory and later Friarscroft Laundry'.*

109

The Regal cinema

The Regal as it looked in 1937

REGAL CINEMA
WYMONDHAM

Proprietor :—   D. F. BOSTOCK

Always a First Class Programme

Times of Performances—

MONDAY to FRIDAY
One Performance   .... 7 p.m.
SATURDAY
Three Performances   .... 2 p.m., 5.30 p.m., & 8.15 p.m.
SUNDAY
One Performance   .... 7 p.m.

CHILDREN NOT ADMITTED

Prices of Admission (Including Tax)—
2/9,   2/3,   1/9,   1/-,   and 10d.

Booking Office Open—

Monday to Friday—
    Mornings, 11.30 to 12.45. Afternoons, 3 to 4.
Saturday—
    Mornings, 11 to 12 Afternoons, 2.30 to 4.
Phone : Wymondham 3149.

Douglas Bostock bought a green field in Friarscroft Lane in 1936 and built the Regal cinema. It was opened by Edwin Gooch, chairman of the UDC in March 1937 with the film 'Swingtime'. Harold Crane was the manager, (with car in next photo), Bert Caley projectionist assisted by Douggie Cranness. Albert Brown was commissionaire. The usherettes were Gwennie Kerrison, Margery Fennell, Mabel Poll and Dorothy Caley. Every performance ended with the National Anthem.

110

In 1937 the Chum's Club began on Saturday afternoons with showings of westerns, cartoons and the 'serial'. During the war years, 1939-45, the Regal provided an escape. There were collections for the war effort and other charities. Sometimes queues went twice round the block and down Friarscroft Lane.

In 1965 Les King became doorman at the Regal and was promoted to manager the following year. Les expanded the activities enjoyed at the Regal to include a café and disco opened in 1969. An American pool table was installed and Bingo started.

In the 1970s Les King started a removal business and left the cinema. It closed for a short time but re-opened in mid 1977. In 1990 the cinema had been open to the public for over 50 years - Les King was manager for 25 of those.

The Regal did eventually close but Michael Armstrong had learned how to operate the projectors and these days he and other enthusiasts run the very popular and successful 'Regal Experience' showing six or more films each year in the Regal building, now the home of the Ex Servicemen's Club.

Brewery Lane

Named after the brewery, which occupied a large site on the right hand side, between Queen Street and the Consort Hotel. Going towards Queen Street are stores and outhouses of properties facing Market Street. They have been described as 'medieval rear-servicing' (John Wilson). Drays came along the road loaded with beer to deliver to pubs in the town and further afield.

Queen Street

This street, originally called New Road, was cut through from the Market Place to Brewery Lane in the 1880s but was probably renamed Queen Street on the occasion of Victoria's Diamond Jubilee in 1897.

The Baptist Church

The Baptists paid £250 for a site at the top of the new road and opened a chapel there in 1897 to seat 250. This is the present schoolroom with a baptistry under the floor. They decided to build a new chapel and a stone laying took place in 1909. Bricks were sold for 5 shillings each to raise money. Miss Lowe said, *'the Baptists used to borrow our water cart to fetch water from the Tiffey for baptisms'*. Michael Marwood remembers attending **Lyndhurst School** in the Baptist schoolroom there during the Second World War and sheltering from bombs in the baptistry under the floor! A trapdoor covered the baptismal pool which could serve as an air-raid shelter. During one air raid incendiary bombs damaged the church and when a bomb was found on the schoolroom roof, children were sent home.

Lyndhurst School

During the 1930s and 40s this private school was run by the Misses Kathleen and Emily Brighton. The playground is now the car park.

Discipline was strict and break-time milk was warmed on a paraffin stove. The school moved into Bridewell Street for a time, before finally moving to the former Wicklewood workhouse. Lyndhurst pupils wore a smart brown uniform and

Lyndhurst School, Wymondham.

Preparatory School for Girls & Boys

All Subjects, Modern Methods. DANCING and MUSIC. Swimming and Tennis

SUCCESSES WITH HONOURS AT THE RECENT ROYAL DRAWING SOCIETY EXAMINATIONS

Distinction and Honour Successes at Associated Board Examinations

Recognised by Board of Education London

For prospectus apply: The Misses Brighton

some residents can recall them around the town in the 1970s.

Photograph of Lyndhurst School, taken on the steps of the Baptist Church, 1951

Front row l to r
Barbara Brighton, Jane Aldridge, Janet Peacock, Richard Blythe, Jennifer Oldfield, Liane Smith, Philip Allcock

2nd row r to l
Mary Rice, Ian Moore, Robert Saunders. Diane Hastings, Peter Philips, Diane Burr, Alistair Brooks, John Lister, Jane Aldridge, Malcolm Cook

3rd row l to r
Jennifer Bunn, Julia Mallett, Frances Brighton, Beverley Baker, ?, Penelope Cooper, Jill Smith, ?, Hastings, Diane Gayton, ? Maurice Dale, JanetCross

4th row r to l
Gillian Wellend, Joanne Semmence, ?, Monica Rackham, Richard Phillips, John Baker, Katherine Semmence, ?, Jean Spinks, Keith Howes

Back row l to r
Joy Pinchen, Julie Frost, Elizabeth Chapman, Diana Elkins, Richard Marwood, Elizabeth Seppings, Guy Millward, ?, Brooks, Glenda Pegnall,

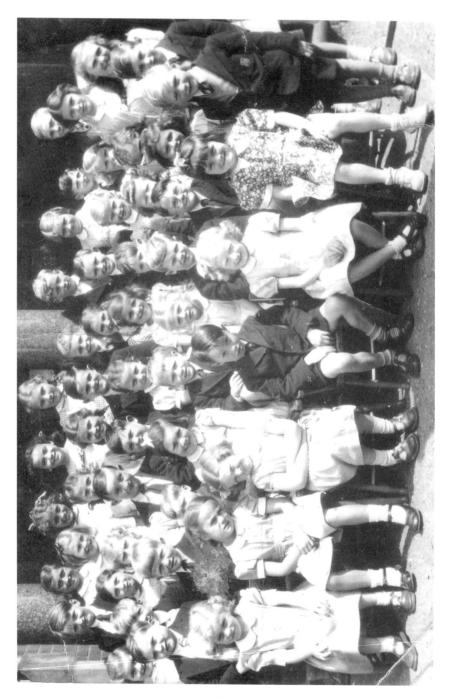

114

Wymondham Brewery

Brewing in Wymondham was an important part of the local economy from the 17th century until the 1890s.

In 1738 **Thomas Randall** a rich Wymondham brewer died. His daughter Ann had married Jeremiah Burroughs I in the 1720s. Ann predeceased her father and his brewery went to his four grandchildren - Jeremiah Burroughs II, Randall Burroughs, Thomas and Thomas Randall III. Jeremiah Burroughs II carried on the brewery until his death in 1767, after which, Randall Burroughs sold the brewing effects and almost all the pubs but not the brewery buildings, to **John Stephenson Cann**. He had inherited his grandfather, John Stephenson's brewery in 1773 and by 1780 had bought the brewery property left to Thomas Randall III as well. **Cann's brewery** established c. 1780, became the foremost in Wymondham and also an important Norfolk brewery.

Map of the town in 1810 showing Cann's and Harvey's breweries

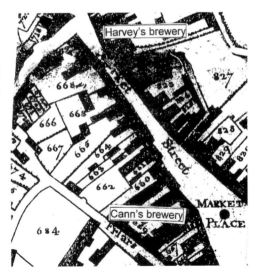

John Stephenson Cann was probably living in the brewery premises by then. There was a house, brewery, malt house, stables and a malt

house yard. These were situated in a large block of property between the present Queen Street and the Consort Hotel. Cann died in 1813 and his son William Robert who was then living in the mansion house in Market Street, succeeded him in the business. In 1824 he went into partnership with John Mitchell, EP Clarke and William Robert Clarke. Cann instructed the latter in brewing and Clarke lived in the mansion house at the brewery; Cann bought Cavick House in 1825. The business was called 'Cann & Clarke, beer and porter brewers and malsters and wine & spirit merchants'. In 1832 they purchased Harvey's brewery. By 1860 William, son of W R Cann had joined them. The latter died in 1867 and Elijah Crozier Bailey his son-in-law, joined the firm.

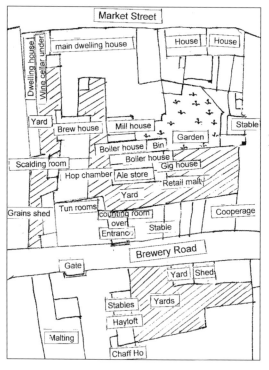

Plan of the brewery c. 1875

In 1872 the brewery was auctioned – it comprised the brewery plant and machinery, malting office, family residence, houses, cottages, 42 pubs and 100 acres. On completion, William Cann and Elijah C. Bailey controlled the company called Cann and Co. The Baileys took complete control in the 1880s and acquired Watton brewery in 1891. Willam Cann had died at Cavick in 1894, still being owed £23,000 by the Baileys. The brewery was sold to Morgans of Norwich in 1894.

A new use for the brewery
In 1896 S D Page converted the brewery buildings to a bass dressing and drafting works to serve its Wymondham and Norwich factories. It served in this capacity until 1921. The brush fibres came in big bales; they were cleaned and dressed and dyed if necessary, in the former brewery vats. It was very smelly work. The prepared fibres were then taken to the brush factories.

The former brewery, leased from Morgan's Brewery Co., Norwich 1896-1921

Part of the old brewery becomes a swimming pool
In 1931 William Smith opened a swimming pool in a huge former beer vat there. **Joan Bunn** had this to say to say about Wymondham's pool:

'You could pay sixpence and stay all day before the war years. People would come from miles around. I particularly remember soldiers arriving by the lorry load for slipper baths. What a luxury that was. When my uncle retired he sold the pool but it soon closed in 1953, It was used by the Norwich Penguins Swimming Club.'

Pupils from Browick Road School, with their teacher William Baker (centre), at the Town swimming pool in the early 1930s

After the pool closed, part of the building became the HQ of the South Norfolk Labour Party for a time.

Chain Entry

At the junction of Brewery Lane and Chandler's Hill is a narrow path which links with Damgate. There are various suggestions as to the origin of its name. However, the most likely explanation seems to be that it was possibly used as a chain measure (22 yards), by the weavers who lived in the houses on the left of the path going towards Damgate.

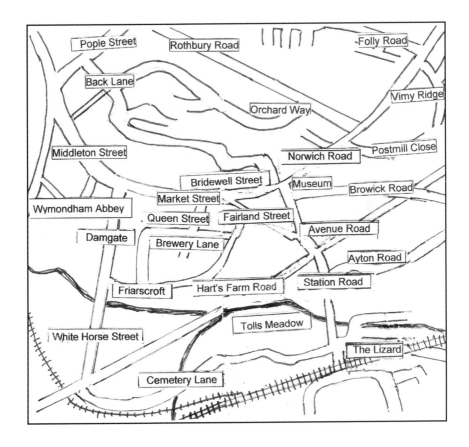

Wymondham Station

Wymondham railway station opened in July 1845 as a stopping point on the line between Norwich and Brandon, providing a link to London via Ely. By 1846 a link to Yarmouth was complete and daily excursions costing 3d (1p) were available. A branch line from Wymondham to East Dereham and Fakenham was opened in 1849, extending to Wells. Another line to Forncett was completed by 1881. This provided a link for North Norfolk traffic with Ipswich and London.

Forncettt station, 1929

The railway station which became an important junction in the eastern region, was a landmark in the town's history, bringing economic and social benefits.

It was a very busy station – some eight or nine trains ran daily on the Wymondham to Dereham line. This necessitated a large work force of some 30 or more. The grandfather of Percy Cobb, station master in the early 1900s recalled how smart they were in their uniform. The station also had a W H Smiths bookstall and refreshment room.

Some memories of Wilfred Coleman, a railway worker:

'I went to work at Wymondham railway station. The station master's house adjoined the station. People would come and sit by the fire in the waiting room in the evening.
I got one free cup of tea in the refreshment room each day.

A boy would go along the train with a trolley selling cups to passengers. They'd give him 6d and tell him to keep the change. Boys also sold the Evening News along the train.

I made sure all the handles on the train doors were shut and there was a lamp at the end of the train. A lot of railwaymen lived on the Lizard. In 1919 some cattle strayed on the line and an engine and wagons were derailed.'

The refreshment room in 1925. Gertrude Lowrie left and Nora Chapman right. They worked a six day week from 7am – 10pm

The station 1924, WH Smith's bookstall in background

Memories of the station during World War Two
Mr Coleman:
'During the Second World War, one of the tracks between Ashwellthorpe and Forncett was used to store explosives. The wagons were grouped in fives where the banks were high. They had military guards and secret messages would be received for their dispatch to various destinations.'
Mrs Beryl Cousins
*'This particular weekend (*after D Day 1944*), my brother and I were walking through the station. We had seen all the ambulances queuing up in Cemetery Lane and I was standing on the station platform. As the train pulled in, I was flabbergasted when they began to unload all the wounded men swathed in bandages and some with what appeared to be burned faces. I was 16 years old and I knew there was a war on, but for the first time, it was brought home to me what war was all about'.*

She is referring to American casualties who would be taken from the station to the Army hospital at Morley.

Mr Wilson
'I left Kiddles and worked at W H Smith & Sons on the railway station book stall and did various paper rounds in the town. I knew most of the station staff. Mr Cobb the station master, Mr Lawn chief clerk (later S/M), Thompson, Bunn, Tyrell, foreman Kidd and Mr Firman were others. I often served the earl of Kimberley who caught the train to London and the notorious vicar of Stiffkey Rev Harold Davison who changed trains at Wymondham. He was a dapper little man who always had the Telegraph and Times. He wore a pin stripe suit with a stiff brimmed trilby.
Mr Elkins had a newsagency in Market Street. He could be seen every morning going to the station with his barrow to meet the 6.40am. He would almost run down the hill all loaded up with newspapers and one morning he almost went into the Tiffey !'

The forecourt of the station 1908, with horse drawn cabs to transport passengers to the King's Head Inn

The coming of railways in the 1840s ended the 'golden age' of coaching and with it, the most colourful period of the King's Head Inn. However, the inn organised cabs to meet every train at Wymondham station. The fare was one shilling.

In the early 20th century, gravel from G R Ayton, gravel merchant, was taken in horse drawn tumbrels to the Silfield side of the station where men would load it into trucks with shovels all day long – over 30 trucks left each day.

The Cemetery
The cemetery rises steeply from the former Love Lane (now **Cemetery Lane**). In 1878 a burial board acquired nine acres of land where two mortuary chapels, a caretaker's lodge and a boundary wall were built at a cost of £2,550. The cemetery opened in 1882.

Opening the cemetery in 1882

A view from Cemetery Lane

A viewing point looking across Tolls Meadow to the Abbey, put up as part of the Tiffey Trail project in 2008.

Station Road
This road was so named after the opening of the station in 1845

The Railway
The inn here was originally called the **Dun Cow** but changed its name to the Railway Commercial Hotel after the station was opened in 1845.

The Lizard
The 12 acres along the Tiffey between the Norwich-Ely line and the first A11 by pass, are in the care of the Lizard Charity whose trustees administer it for the general benefit and enjoyment of the people of Wymondham.

There has been much speculation about the meaning of the word 'Lizard'. It has been suggested that it came from Lazar House, a hospital for lepers or Leziate, an open field or leaze. In 1684 Edmund Ellis's lands are described as being next to the common pasture of Wymondham called Lyzer.

A dispute about the Lizard Charity

In the 1720s there was a dispute about the purpose of the Lizard Charity. It was said that the original deed had been lost in the fire of 1615 and that the charity was for the poor of Wymondham. The Commissioners appointed to decide on this, decreed that this **was** the true purpose. Some townspeople did not agree with this and a Mr Wright brought an action in the Court of Chancery in 1723. The court decided that **every** inhabitant of the town who had three cows, could put them to graze on the Lizard.

Tom Turner, town clerk, - some thoughts about Lizard residents during the 1940s &50s:
'They were always a bit on their own with their own shop. Harry Warnes' father had the shop and did a grocery round in

the country on Saturdays – he was called the 'Saturday man'.
The Percivals carried on the shop. I won't say the elder son was
a film star but he played quite a leading part in some films in
the early days. Kenny Percival and his elder brother played the
piano well and would entertain in public houses.'

The stone pit
Mr W R Wilson
'During World War One, the German POWs worked in the large
stone pit in Station Road and carted stone to the station'.

Tom Alderton
'My father worked in the stone pit in Station Road for 5s a week.'

The Aytons
They were a family of gravel merchants and road builders. Their
business was based in **Ayton Road**, which is named after them.
Now the May Gurney company occupies the site.

Mrs Cyril Ayton's memories of the family business:
'They used shovels and picks. A side track at the station
was used to load gravel. Charles started with five men and
two horse tumbrels. Malcolm and Cyril Ayton started Ayton
Asphalt when their father died. About 1930 they got into
trouble because they had put all their money into Aytons and
brought a man from Bristol to teach them how to make tarmac.
During the Depression all contracts were stopped and they
lost everything. Charles died in 1928 and May Gurney bought
up the business. The gravel pits were running out so they
turned to asphalt.
Charles R Ayton dined with King Edward VII in Norwich.
When the King drove from Quidenham to Norwich through
Wymondham, a triumphal arch was built for him to pass
under'.

Tiffey Bridge & Tolls Meadow

In the decade before Kett's Rebellion (1549), Robert Kett owned between 40-50 acres of land including six in the vicinity of Tiffey Bridge, known then as Tyfford Bridge. He also had three acres known as Tyffin Meadow. This could have been what is now known as Tolls Meadow. On the other hand, the name Tolls Meadow could be linked to the Toll family in the 18th century.

2, Station Road - Gas House,

Approaching the town from the direction of the station, the house is just before the traffic lights on the left.

In 1892 **Charles Dawson Banham** came to live here with his family when he was appointed manager of the town's gas works at the age of 28. Gas had first come to Wymondham in 1848 and until 1930 the town's houses were lit by gas.

The Banham family c. 1900, outside Gas House. Ethel, who later married Edwin Gooch, is on the left of the back row

The Banhams were devout Primitive Methodists and it was at the local chapel that they met the Gooch family whose head, Simon, ran a smithy in Fairland Street. In 1914 Charles Banham's second daughter Ethel, married Edwin Gooch. The couple were early activists in the recently founded Labour Party and soon became prominent in local and county politics.

Charles Banham was active in the wider community too. He became a trustee of Wymondham Primitive Chapel, Treasurer of Wymondham Liberal and Radical Association, a leading figure in the Wymondham Miniature Rifle Club and a member of the Oddfellows Friendly Society.

Charles and Edwin both appear in this photo of the '**Muscular Methodists**' 1912. They were clearing an orchard which was behind the Town Green chapel, for a recreation ground.

Ethel Gooch 1887- 1953, Wymondham's first 'first lady'
Ethel trained as a teacher and after her marriage to Edwin in 1914, she returned to Wymondham to join the staff of Browick Junior School, becoming headmistress in 1918. After the birth of her son Michael in 1923 she became increasingly involved in politics. She was one of the first women to take an active part in the Labour party,

128

helping to set up a women's group in the South Norfolk branch. In due course she served on rural, urban, district and county councils. She was a county councillor serving for 22 years, six as an alderman. She was also a JP. and a member of 16 committees, two of which she chaired and served as vice chair of another.

She was elected to Wymondham Urban District Council in 1937, becoming its first woman chair in 1951.

Portrait of Ethel Gooch in the 1930s

During the Second World War she and Edwin welcomed two evacuees into their home and Ethel became even busier helping on the Home Front with various welfare schemes in the town and county. The WI of which she was president, was very active and she coined the slogan *'Grow your own food and cook what you grow.'*

In 1940 she helped to set up a local branch of the Women's Voluntary Service later becoming its president. This organisation liaised with WI and gave help to evacuees, servicemen and other groups in need. She started a house-to-house collection for families bombed out of their homes in London

After Ethel's sudden death in 1953, the council stood for a minute's silence in her honour. At her funeral many groups and organisations were represented, including the Labour Party, the National Union of Agricultural Workers (NUAW), Norfolk County Council, the County Nursing Association, British Legion, Red Cross, Housing Committee, Social Services, Magistrates, WI, schools and churches. Some distinguished figures in public life were also present such as, Lincoln Ralphs County Education Officer, Sam Peel Chairman of NCC and Morgan Phillips Secretary of the Labour Party.

The many tributes following her death testify to the high regard in which she was held. She was a woman of strong character, combining courage and honesty with tolerance and sympathy. She had made a huge contribution to social welfare in Wymondham and Norfolk and played an important part in the growth of the Labour Party in this area.

Fairland Street – takes its name from the 'Fairstead' or Fairland. The street was originally called Fairstead Street.

The Fairland

This small green space is a remnant of extensive c o m m o n land in the 16th century. Blomefield says Kett had enclosed some land

near the 'Fairstead'. Was it near here that the incident which marked the start of the rebellion took place when rioters bribed by Kett's enemy Flowerdew, pulled down Kett's fences ? Then he recognised the injustice of enclosure and helped the rioters by pulling down his own fences, offering to lead them in a protest.

This area of land was used for thrice yearly fairs, a right granted to the town by King Stephen in the 12ᵗʰ century.

In 1919 Edwin Gooch organised a big political demonstration on the Fairland in support of the Labour Party. It was attended by 1500 people and Lord Kimberley, the first Labour peer, was present. In 1920 George Edwards the first Labour candidate, captured south Norfolk for the party in the by-election. Gooch was Edwards' political agent and was credited as the 'organiser of victory.'

Planting the trees on the Fairland alongside
Avenue Road c. 1920s

In 1940 the Fairland was one of ten places listed as a site for a public air raid shelter.

The Fairland Church

This is the oldest nonconformist church in Wymondham. Its origins lay in the 17ᵗʰ century. This was a time when there was turmoil for the Church of England because Puritans wanted to reform the church along Presbyterian lines which would mean the abolition of bishops and independent congregations.

During the regime of Archbishop Laud in the 1630s, Puritans, including some in Wymondham, were forced to emigrate to escape persecution.

However during the Commonwealth of the 1650s under Cromwell, there was tolerance of Puritan groups. The religious exiles returned and founded the first Congregational churches in Yarmouth and Norwich. By now Puritans were using 'lecturers' or preachers in their congregations.

John Money, 'a fervant' Puritan preacher

He had a reputation as an effective preacher and in 1644 he was appointed as 'lecturer' at the Abbey church indicating that he was not a religious extremist. However, in 1646 he was among several men who discussed the possible founding of a Congregational or Independent church in Wymondham. This was eventually started in 1652.

When the monarchy was restored in 1660 in the person of Charles II, tolerance of religious nonconformity ceased. The new government was determined to pass laws to try and suppress the congregational churches. Money's name appears on a return of ejected ministers as *'John Money, MA, vicar of Wymondham, ejected in 1661'*.

By 1664 it was illegal for Puritan assemblies or conventicles to meet. However they continued to do so and in the Norwich diocese there were some 80 or more conventicles by 1667.

The largest group of religious dissenters was in Wymondham where Puritanism continued to flourish in part due to the influence and preaching of John Money.

However, in 1672 Charles II relaxed the religious laws and allowed licensed meetings in definite places addressed by specific preachers in private houses. So preachers like Money now had free reign to promote their ideas. As a result he took out a licence to preach and there were four houses licensed in the town.

Money died in 1673 with a reputation for learning and admired for his *'fervant, frequent and exact preaching'.*

The first 'Independent church' gets a permanent Meeting House.
A meeting house in Wymondham was funded by Roger Gay, a deacon of the Fairland church, on his own land c.1715-16. His legacy allowed the trustees of the church to use the income from several plots of land outside Wymondham as well as two wheelwright's shops, some cottages, barns and meadowland, to build a meeting house facing the fairstead or Fairland. The building was about half the size of the Fairland Church today.

An early photo of the Fairland Church
before the changes made in 1879

In 1848 a school was built under the auspices of the British & Foreign Society for nonconformist churches. This involved demolishing some of the older barns, stables and wheelwright's shops. It was located next to the greatly enlarged church. This would have catered for 200 children paying 2d a week for reading writing and arithmetic and 4d if they wanted geometry, geography and history. £200 was collected from the townspeople for the building and a master was paid £40 a year. However, there were never more than 50 pupils and the trustees had to dig into their own pockets.

In the 1870s, state or Board schools came along and the Fairland Church school building was used by private schools, the Sunday school and for social events. At the time of World War One it was extended and became the Fairland Hall looking much as it does today.

Peace celebrations in front of the Fairland Church, 1919. The former school building is on the left

In September 1938 the town bellman announced that gas masks would be distributed at Fairland Hall in anticipation of a gas attack.

The meadowland from Gay's legacy, became the site of Hall & Palmer's sale yard until 1977. The Job Centre and telephone exchange were built on adjoining land in the 1960s and the Health Centre for the town, was completed in 1983.

Some memories of the Fairland Church
George Duffield
'*Mrs Bartram would ask my mother if I would help at the Saturday evenings held at Fairland Hall or school room. I had to go and get whatever my part was there. There were five in a team, Marie Standley, Doris Kidman, Minnie Thompson, Roy Gooch and me. We had to learn our parts and would go to Mrs B twice a week for rehearsals. When I was at home my mother would take the other parts. These pleasant Saturday evenings were held during the winter months and Mr Walter Lane was in charge.*'

Eva Chapman
'*During Gun Week in 1942, the Market Place was filled with guns and soldiers. You could buy certificates for 15s. They would take old aluminium in. Railings were taken from library and Fairland Church. I was glad to get back to the Fairland Church which had been taken over by the army. Just before the war there were concerts there with Sunday school children. We had a concert and obtained curtains which would be put in front and all around the back of the stage. After the war we never did find them – they had burned benches and chairs to keep warm. It was a job to get back to normality.*'

The Fairland Diner This property on the corner of one of Wymondham's interesting little yards, was from the late 1890s, a confectioner's, tobacconist and fancy goods shop with refreshment rooms as well. It was run by Sidney Gooch, second son of Simon the blacksmith. After Sidney died in 1909, his wife Rose continued with the shop and advertised 'Parties catered for'. The business provided a valuable service for visitors to the Fairland Street sale ground.

The yard next to the Fairland diner
The two 16th or 17th century cottages in the yard next to the diner, once belonged to the Fairland Church. Some Wymondham

residents remember two large trees in the yard and a pump and well which served the cottages and other buildings. Piped water did not come to the town until 1932. There was also a saw pit - a large hole in the ground where two men operated a large saw.

In the yard is this building with its dentil cornice and tumbelling. It appears on the 1810 map and is similar in style to other 18th century and earlier Wymondham buildings.

The Colmans seem to have worked there as builders, plumbers, painters & glaziers from 1845. It was said that woodwork to the left of the double doors came from Wymondham Abbey.

It was acquired by Skipper and Bartram in the 1890s for their building business which developed into the undertakers' at 11, Fairland Street. From 1925 the business

SKIPPER & BARTRAM,
Carpenters and Builders
FAIRLAND ST., WYMONDHAM.

Coffins made Funerals undertaken
on the most reasonable terms

Machine Planing and Ripping
FOR THE TRADE

concentrated on carpentry and undertaking and eventually moved across the road to the current chapel of rest.

Inside the building fixed to the wall and looking as if it has been there since the time of the notice, is an announcement of the Wymondham School Board School elections of 1878 and the results of the election in 1887.

5, Fairland Street, Clements & Sons, Ironmongers and much more !
One of the oldest independent shops in the town

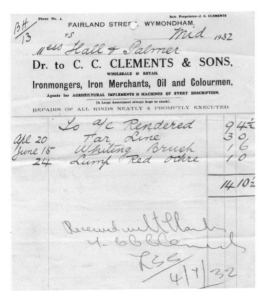

By 1883 Cubitt Cornelius Clements was an ironmonger, and oil and colour man. He was also a dealer in farming implements. By 1896 he had another shop on the corner of Market Place and Bridewell Street. Underneath the sign on the present charity shop is the wonderful original Clements shop sign.

Around 1900, Newton, Pollock and Wilson occupied the premises now known as the Handbag & Leather Shop (3, Fairland Street) which later housed the East Anglian Trustee Savings Bank.

F W Myhill & Son

This property was originally the Woolpack. At first it was licensed only to sell beer, but by 1840 it had a full licence when the building shown in the picture believed to have been used later by the Salvation Army, and now Yum Yums, was the pub's stables.

It was sold by Cann & Clarke in 1894 to Morgans and finally closed in 1966. It was then bought by F W Myhill & Son who had opened in the street in 1937, where Wardrobes (20, Fairland Street), is now.

24 & 26, Fairland Street, Frank Cross Antiques
This shop was adjacent to the block of flats, number 28

16, Fairland Street, The Old Forge This has been used by various retailers, but is currently empty.

In 1876 **Simon Gooch** (1842-1912)**,** a blacksmith who had come to Wymondham in 1862, started up on his own in 1876 in this property as a smith and machinist. By 1879 he was listed in Kellys Directory as a farrier. The Gooch family became one of the best known in Wymondham for many decades. He and his wife Ellen had 11 children, some of whom followed him into the business, but some like Edwin, did not. Simon was an ardent Liberal, a lifelong non-conformist and a regular attender at the Methodist Town Green church. But he also seems to have had some sympathies for the new socialist ideas and the trade union movement, which were spreading in the 1890s-1900s.
There is a story that he rescued **Kett's Oak** from decline and perhaps renewed the iron railings round the tree. At his funeral he was referred to an ' *man, of integrity and lover of fair play &*

justice..... humble and devout. His customary habit was that of the lowly heart'. These qualities were echoed in the character of his most famous son, Edwin who benefited from a stable and loving family with clear moral values.

Fairland Street early 1900s – members of the Gooch family can be seen outside their workshop on the left

Simon's son **Albert,** continued with the business until 1918, when he sold it to the Reeve family.

The last blacksmith to work at these premises was **George Reeve** who retired in 1992

'Our trade as we know it has disappeared. People do not know what a blacksmith is. I have worked all my life and never taken a holiday because of the obligation I feel towards my customers. We used to shoe horses and farmers would bring in everything they could for us to repair rather than buy new.'

dr Pomeroy (Re Burial Board   June 29   192 9

Dr. to CHAS. E. REEVE,

Shoeing Smith and General Machinist.

RUBBER TYREING DONE ON THE PREMISES.

AGENT FOR HUNTON & SONS' PLOUGHS, &c.

Edwin Gooch 1889-1964, from blacksmith's boy and trade unionist, to MP and chairman of the Labour Party

The youngest son of Simon the blacksmith and his wife Ellen, he did not like working in his father's forge and started work at the Norwich Mercury as a printer in 1907, then became a journalist rising to chief sub editor.

Outside the Gooch forge c. 1906.

Edwin is second left, looking a little uncomfortable.

Simon Gooch is on the far right.

Simon Gooch on left with Edwin looking very dapper 2nd left
and his mother far right c. 1910

The Banham family c. 1913 with Edwin on the back row far right,
behind Ethel Banham seated front c. 1913
In 1914 Edwin and Ethel married

In 1918 the South Norfolk Labour Party began and Edwin was one of its founding members. By 1922 he was a JP and had been elected to Norfolk County Council, the Rural District Council and Wymondham Parish Council.

He was increasingly active in politics serving as George Edwards' political agent. He was also drawn to the plight of the farm workers and supported the Great Norfolk Strike of 1923 against wage cuts becoming a member of the strike committee.

The striking farm workers march through Wicklewood - Gooch is in the front row on right

In 1930 he was elected President of the National Union of Agricultural Workers (NUAW), a post he held until 1964. The union did much to improve the lot of farm workers. In promoting its cause, Edwin became known as the 'farm worker's friend'.

After George Edwards retired from politics in 1924, Edwin was chosen as Labour candidate for South Norfolk, but failed to capture the seat in 1931. Even so his influence in the Labour Party continued to grow – he attended conferences and told the party at Brighton in 1935 that 'farm workers' votes will capture the countryside'. He continued to be active in the affairs of the town becoming Chairman of Wymondham Parish Council, later the Urban District Council in 1935. Water and sewage projects were started and the old horse drawn fire engine was replaced by a Dennis engine. Edwin and Ethel campaigned to clean up the Tiffey, put a footpath on Damgate Bridge and build a by-pass which would provide jobs for men in the depressed stone industry

During the Second World War, he was a key figure on the Home Front as Chairman of the Wymondham Invasion Committee and Civil Co-ordinator for Wymondham, testimony to his organising ability.

In 1944 he was awarded the CBE for services to agriculture. In the same year he was chosen as Labour candidate for North Norfolk.

In the 1945 election he won the seat for Labour and held it till 1963.

By now he was a respected and influential member of the party and was elected to the Labour Party National Executive. He mixed with the Prime Minister Attlee and senior Cabinet ministers. Attlee came to Norfolk to visit George Edwards' grave at Fakenham, Ernest

144

Bevin, Foreign Secretary, visited Wymondham for a political rally and Herbert Morrison Home Secretary, was a guest at a NUAW dinner.

In 1955 Edwin was elected to the key position of Chairman of the Labour Party. The blacksmith's boy from rural Norfolk was now at the head of a great industrial party.

Edwin Gooch with Prime Minister Attlee

Edwin Gooch died in 1964 and his funeral in the Methodist Church which had been so influential in his development as a boy and young man, was followed by a memorial service in the Abbey Church.

Pat Salmon a great niece, wrote:

'Uncle Ted's funeral was very moving with all those farm workers singing their hearts out. Afterwards we progressed to the cemetery via Fairland Street with the union banner carried before. People stood in doorways, men with their hats off, as the procession passed. It was very moving. I wept.'

The Times described Edwin as ' *a sturdy champion of farm workers, moderate…co-operative rather than confrontational and competitive…. who devoted as much time and energy to Norfolk affairs as beyond'.*

There were many tributes from a huge number of groups and organisations in which he served. Edwin Gooch had made a massive contribution to Wymondham, Norfolk and the nation through his work as a councillor, trade unionist and politician. He was a selfless servant of the common man.

6a, Fairland Street, formerly the Crown public house
This pub stood on the corner of Friarscroft and Fairland Street. It closed in 1981.

Market Place

4, Market Place, Anchor House
The frontage of this property is late 18th or early 19th century. The rear part of the premises dates even earlier. In the cellar is a beam which was perhaps re-used after the Great Fire of 1615.

6, Market Place, the Cross Keys

This inn dates from the 16th century and its original Tudor timbered frontage can be seen on the left. The photograph also shows the Cross Keys before it acquired its mock Tudor front, added in the 1960s.

In 1900, Youngs, Crawshaw and Young purchased the building next door including Harvey's bakery. Fred Tillett the fishmonger had it for a time but it was eventually incorporated into the pub and given a 'mock Tudor' frontage.

The Tudor frontage of the Cross Keys can be seen
in the background

Harvey's bakery, where Mr Bunn learned his trade before setting up on his own.
'Bunn was the last baker to use a horse for delivering.'
(Tubby Fulcher)

From the 1800s the present estate agent, was Skoulding's chemist shop until it was acquired by Laycock, who ran it as a grocer and pork butcher by 1900. In 1913 William Bunn bought it for his bakery business.

Standley's Antiques shop - the Olde Curiosity Shop, 1920s.

Many generations of the Standley family ran an antiques business in these premises on the Market Place.

Queen Street

This attractive building near the corner of Queen Street and Market Street, sadly no longer here, was used by the **Ex-Servicemen's Club.**
It was supported by people like Jacob Standley, Harry Clarke the grocer and George Allison the auctioneer.

Market Street

Numbers 40-32, Market Street

On the site of the present shops from Paper Wishes to Savers, were the former Cann brewery buildings. Right on the corner of Queen Street and the Market Place was the Queen's Arms. This pub was described by Miss Lowe as the brewery's '*jug and bottle*' department. It was known as '*Up the Steps*' and closed c. 1910.

Lost buildings in Market Street

Next to the Queen's Arms was the former part of the brewery complex which housed the Men's Club.

Wymondham
Men's Club
MARKET STREET
(Next Post Office)

Members admitted at 17 years

Billiards & Snooker
OPEN TO NON-MEMBERS

A COMFORTABLE READING
& GAMES ROOM
Containing Daily and Weekly Periodicals
always open

Annual Subscription 10/-

Debating Society Meeting every month.
Full particulars from the Steward
2 Well Furnished Rooms for Hire
suitable for Meetings, Whist Drives, etc.
Whist Tables and Cards available.

The Men's Club can be seen in the front right of this photo

Tubby Fulcher tells how he started out at Briton Brush in 1921 as a 'dogsbody' at the old brewery where Somerfields was, (now Savers). The brush factory used part of the brewery buildings for dyeing and he had to '*take the dyed stuff to the Briton*'.

Miss Lowe describes how there were very nice Georgian houses next to the **Post Office** which moved from the Market Place into part of the old brewery.

Every night before 11pm Miss Lowe described a great noise when the horse drawn wagon from Dereham arrived to collect the mailbags at the Post Office and take them to the station to join the *'up mail'*. The men then went to the Railway Tavern and would rest the horses until the *'down mail'* arrived at about 2am and then return to Dereham. There were three postal deliveries daily – early morning, noon and afternoon!

George Duffield's memories of working at the Post Office

'I left Browick Road school at 14 and started at the Post Office as a telegraph boy next day! I went to school on Monday morning and stood at the desk and the headmaster Mr Sparkes said "what do you want"? and I said "I want to leave sir". "Have you got a job?" "Yes, I start at the P.O. at 9am".

I was there six months and cycled around delivering telegrams (over a two mile area) up Norwich Rd as far as Old Oak. I worked for 6 months and then did not pass the doctor's medical. The Postmaster lived next door to the main entrance to the Post Office. You went up some steps to his home. I went there one morning at 8am. My Sunday school teacher was on duty - she handed me the telegram and said

"Kimberley Hall" so I got on my bike. My hours were 8am-6pm or 9am-7pm. I got my telegram and went to deliver it. When I got back I was handed another telegram – I had to walk as the one bike was in use. When I returned, the Postmaster wanted to see me and asked me why I did not pump the water at his house. There was no telephone then. What was most important - water or the telegram?'

Post Office workers in front of the Post Office c.1900

A new Post office opened in a purpose built building in Middleton Street in 1940 and in 1943, the **Mary Elizabeth Tea Rooms** moved into the former Post Office premises from their shop in Bridewell Street which had opened in 1939. Both owners were called Mary Elizabeth.

It could not have been easy to succeed in wartime with rationing etc but their home made fare was popular with local traders, shoppers coming in from the villages, visitors to the town and the Americans! At a time when the A11 ran along the street there was also trade from passing customers. The tea room was sold in 1949 and it continued until 1958.

In 1963 the old brewery buildings, which included the former tea room were pulled down and new ones (the present shops) were built.

The house next to the former Post Office, now the Children's Society charity shop, (number 30 Market Street), became W A Ogden's chemists shop, having been a private house in Miss Lowe's (b. 1893) time. Mr Ogden gave his name to Ogden Close; he served the town faithfully for many years.

"Mary Elizabeth"

TEA ROOMS . . . . . .
(Proprietress : M. E. Nixon)

MORNING COFFEE
LUNCHEONS
AFTERNOON TEAS

Home made Cakes our Speciality

MARKET PLACE, WYMONDHAM
Phone : 2215

Number 28, Market Street, The Consort Hotel, Memories of a doctor's daughter, Mary Lowe b. 1893

'My father Dr George Lowe, came to Wymondham in the 1880s to take over a practice run by Dr Bush who lived where Barclay's Bank is now. My father stayed there until Semmence of Middleton Street built our house. My father married in 1891. He employed a cook, house maid and page boy. When the boy became too big to be a page boy he worked in the stable.'

This was the building that preceded the present one which was built for Dr Lowe. The property now occupied by the Children's Charity and formerly Ogden's chemist, can be seen on the left.

The Consort Hotel was once the house used by Dr Lowe and later generations of doctors until the new Health Centre was opened on the site of the former sale yard opposite the Bridewell in 1983. Mary Lowe was born here.

Mary's childhood memories

'As a child I wore dresses and a pinafore with frill, a long coat and boots. We had loads of underclothes. I wanted to wear a vest instead of combinations and I won eventually but had to wear a flannel petticoat.

From our drawing room I saw a bear at the George and Dragon pub next to the King's Head, dancing round a pole.

Of course, I remember the Boer War and the relief of Mafeking celebrations (1899). Everyone illuminated their houses with strips of wood with candles on in their windows. They would light them and it was very effective but not very safe. There was singing and dancing in the street. Several men went from Wymondham to the war.

I remember them coming back by train and everyone wanted to shake hands with them in the street - I was about seven years old.

Jessie Harvey the Town Crier, advertised concerts and 'Lost and Found' items outside our house.

Queen Victoria

I can just remember the sports for Queen Victoria's Diamond Jubilee in 1897. They were held on King's Head Meadows and there were bicycle races, hurdles, children's cycle races and obstacle races. On the Kings Head side, people sat on wagonettes. Opposite was a grandstand with hard seats. Next to it was the president's tent where we had tea and were entertained.

People even came down from London for the races.

'When Queen Victoria died (1901), there was six weeks mourning.
My mother was Miss Patty Pomeroy and my grandfather a solicitor in Vicar Street. I was told never to repeat things I heard or say who went into the office. In 1893 the first gas main was laid in Vicar Street which used to have a cobbled path.'

Visiting patients

'When my father visited patients, a coachman in livery and a top hat waited outside in the cart but sometimes he rode his horse. For night calls, a cart would be sent for the doctor. Usually one person in a village did it for everyone. No telephones, meant messages were brought on foot or by cart.

My father wore a top hat and overcoat when he made visits in the town. When Dr David Hughes (the other doctor in the town) *retired, his son Maurice, took over and he and my father decided to wear bowler hats instead. There was no NHS then and home remedies were used. The doctor was paid once a year in cash and patients paid into clubs like the Odd Fellows or the Foresters - a kind of insurance. At the local factories there were many accidents as regulations were not so strict then. Doctors were on duty 24 hours a day and also did post mortems.*

When the motor car came, both doctors had one – but there was no hood if it rained. They attended patients in Forncett, Spooner Row, Barnham Broom, Ketteringham, Morley and Wicklewood. My father attended the workhouse there twice a week. Doctors did their own dispensing then, but when the NHS came in, they had trouble getting patients to go to the chemist for their medicine.
There were no telephones; if people wanted a doctor they sent a telegram – 12 words for 6d. I remember the phone coming and the doctors groaned!'

Getting about

'I had two governesses and then went to Norwich. Some of the older children went to Norwich schools by rail. They cycled or walked or went by pony trap to the station. They put their bikes in a shed which the caretaker of the cemetery had, for 6d a week. It was 1/2d return to Norwich by train – we had season tickets and there were no buses.

My father had a dogcart, then a pony cart and later a brougham. I remember going to Norwich in the dog cart. Two carrier's carts went three times a week to Norwich. There were cabs between Wymondham and the station run by the King's Head and Mallows (a cab business). It was 1/- to the station.. The roads were dusty and a sprinkler went round with little boys following ! It was kept in a yard opposite the Windmill in Norwich Road with a steam roller and equipment. I was the second lady driver in Wymondham and drove my father about in an open car. We'd dress up with veils to keep our hats on.'

Remembering the Abbey and a ghost story

'As regards the Abbey, the Rev Canon Eden was the last person to be buried in the churchyard with special permission, as it had been closed in 1898. I remember his funeral and also the box pews and I could not see over the top. You rented your pew and there were crimson cotton cushions on them. We were told of a ghost on the west tower. A hooded figure of a monk is supposed to walk around the top of the tower. Somebody found out that it was only seen when the moon was in a certain way and cast a shadow. That spoiled the fun.'

Military matters

'There was a drill hall between Mrs Knighton's and Tuddenham's butcher's shop. Sgt Major Moore was the recruiting sergeant. The hall was the HQ of the 4th Battalion of the Norfolk Regt (Volunteers). Each Wednesday they would march up the town headed by a brass band and the officers. My father was their surgeon captain. They wore their red coats 'and blue trousers with the red stripes, and went to

156

drill on King's Head Meadow. Everyone watched them go up and come back. Once a year they went to Yarmouth for two weeks on camp. My father went and took his coachman with him as his batman.

When father died in 1914, another doctor bought the practice – we stayed three months to show him around. I left Wymondham aged 21 wanting to be a doctor but my father died just at the wrong time and I couldn't go because of the money. However, he wouldn't have heard of a woman doctor. So I went to Norwich to train as a masseuse but couldn't finish my training because mother became ill.'

The Old Fire Station

The site to build the old fire station was given to the town by Mrs Julia de Roubigne Beevor Clarke (1806-1894). A fire brigade committee was formed in 1880 to set up a volunteer fire brigade for Wymondham and to purchase two fire engines – a 22 man and a 12 man pump.

The old fire station, 2nd building on the left

157

Miss Lowe's memories of the Fire Brigade:

'The members of the Fire Brigade were all volunteers. The engine was horse drawn by cab horses. Water had to be pumped from the Tiffey. Volunteers would be paid so much an hour for 'pumping up'.

The Wymondham Fire Brigade's 12 man pump in 1905

In 1935 the manual engine was replaced by a Dennis Ace self-propelled pump. At the Wymondham carnival in 1936 the brigade gave a demonstration in which Mrs Standley was 'rescued' from a burning structure and 200 gallons of burning oil were put out in 10 seconds.

During the Second World War there were three sub-stations, a garage in Whitehorse Street, the old drill hall and possibly one on

Norwich Common. The old swimming bath was kept filled with water, for emergencies.

Members of the wartime Fire Brigade, 1939, left to right:
H Ringer, B Woods, F Glasspoole, R Long, B Howlett, E Smith, P Wharton, F Harwood, T Williamson, F Hireson, A Banham, J Thompson, B Dover, R Cullum

The brigade was on standby in the war years for 1,542 air raid warnings, assisting when Gaymers in Attleborough and the Lizard were bombed. Furthermore, it helped the military at American crashes at Crown Farm, Deopham and Morley Hall in 1944 when Fred Harwood and Fred Smith were injured. It also assisted at Morley when a Halifax bomber crashed and two men were rescued. When they attended a chimney fire at the doctor's house it cost Dr Gaynor 2.6d a man.

After the war the old fire station closed and moved to its present site on London Road. The old manual engine is kept there.

Wharton's Lane
This lane, next to the fire station, was named after the Wharton family, who had a butcher's business in the town.

Peter Wharton's memories:

'I relayed messages between firemen telling them to put up the water pressure. Shifts were about three hours and we were paid 2/- a month for using our own bikes. During the blitz I went to Caleys -there was so much combustible material there and chocolate was running everywhere !

I remember sleeping overnight in a Nissen hut on Chandler's Hill where the car park is now, with a tortoise stove and Frank Glasspoole's 'wellies'.

There were two bombing incidents I recall; one was when an enemy plane went along the railway line, the other was when incendiary bombs were dropped on the Baptist Chapel roof.'

Peter's time as a volunteer fireman ended in 1942 when he joined the army.

12/14 Market Street, Wharton's butchers (now Wymondham Motorist Centre)

This photo shows what is now the entrance to **Wharton's Court** with double doors near right, and you can just see part of the frontage of Kerridge's butcher's shop next door - very near right. Arthur Kerridge came to the Market Street shop in 1884 and though

160

he owned Ivy Green Farm on the London Road, he lived at the shop. In Wharton's Court there was a slaughter house.

Memories of Leslie Kerridge, (son of Arthur) :
'We were registered to slaughter animals who came from farms in local auctions. If we bought animals at the Saturday cattle market (in Norwich) *we would drive them along Newmarket Road to Wymondham. If we bought late in the day we would put them on the train to Wymondham. In summer we went to Acle market to get cattle off the marshes. We had ice boxes and bought a cart of ice at a time and there was sawdust on the floor.'*

Cushing's Yard in 1893, by Henry Cushing, a noted local photographer. In 1996 this yard was redeveloped into Wharton's Court by the Wymondham architect, Peter Codling.

The Wharton's took over the Market Street shop in 1938 to add to their shops in Damgate and Town Green. When it closed in 1990, the family business had been in the town for 100 years. Peter Wharton carried on the traditions of courtesy and service with the old style sawdust on the floor and chopping blocks – greatly missed by his former customers.

6 Market Street – the Griffin (now Dove's Boutique)

This former inn may be another example of a Wymondham building which survived the fire of 1615, at least in part. In a room in the back range is an example of a 15th or early 16th century deep roll moulding. The photo shows the former inn, 2nd from the right.
The carriage entrance was used by the Mail coach daily from the 1830s, on its journeys between Norwich and London, as well as local carriers.

In the early 20th century William Bowden came from Attleborough at the request of the owners Morgan's Brewery, and set up his builder's yard behind the inn.

2, Market Street, Clarke & Co (now Geo. R Reeve)
On the right of this photo of Market Street in the 1940s, is the shop founded by Edward 'Ginger' Clarke in 1871. Harry Clarke, his son, took over c. 1920 and the shop continued until his death in 1969. An evacuee Alice Keep, recalls being registered there for food rations during the Second World War.

Miss Lowe's description of Clarke & Co
'The shop that is now George Reeve, was the grocer and drapers of 'Ginger' Clarke. He was always called 'Ginger' but when I remember him, he was grey. There was a nice showroom upstairs for fashions. Downstairs, groceries were sold on one side and drapery the other.'

Clarke's was like a 1950s department store in miniature, selling fabrics, bed linen, carpets, curtains and children's clothes etc. Groceries were delivered in Wymondham and the surrounding villages by trade bike before the war and after 1945, by van.

After Harry Clarke died, this wonderful part of Wymondham's shopping history, finally closed. Fortunately Geo. R Reeve took

163

over the property and used it as a bookshop, stationers and printing works.

Damgate
This ancient street may have got its name as the road leading to the dam of the water mill. From the Domesday Book of 1086, we know that before and after the Norman Conquest there were at least two watermills in Wymondham.

In 1417 Richard Kett, the great grandfather of Robert, had a house in this street.

Damgate was the gateway to the town from the west. Before the 20th century by-passes, it was part of the A11 and the scene of many a traffic jam. The street has been covered in great detail in 'Looking back at Damgate'.

Middleton Street – the street in the middle of the town between Market Street and Town Green.

7, Middleton Street, Caius House
Caius House, now Jarrold Home Furnishings, is a stately Georgian house built in 1746 by Jeremiah Burroughs a landowner who married Ann Randall, daughter of wealthy Wymondham brewer Thomas Randall. When Charles Bird lived there in the 1930s a private bowling club played on the rear lawn. In addition to the lovely garden, there was a first floor conservatory. This can still be seen today.

One of the many evacuees who came to the town during the Second World War was lucky enough to be placed with the family in Caius House and enjoyed her time there.

Memories of Mary Carpenter, nee Bailey, an evacuee
'We left our homes in Gravesend at 5.30am on 3 September 1939 and boarded the 'Golden Daffodil' - never have so many people been so sea-sick. On arriving at Wymondham, three years of a totally different life began for me. We were in a class

The rear of Caius House showing the garden
and the conservatory

-room and my friend and I both 13, were nearly the last to be looked over and chosen by the good folk of Wymondham. We were taken in by a wonderful couple called Jessie and Charlie Bird who had a shop in Middleton Street, called Caius House. Uncle Charlie made furniture and Aunty Jessie sold china chamber pots, tea pots, jugs and tea services. We were allowed to help in the shop and plane or rub down furniture. They had a bowling green as well and our job was to roll the lawn each day. Later on, part of the house was taken over as an officers' mess and the batmen lived up the top stairs. We shared the food left after the officers had eaten.'

9, 11 & 13, Middleton Street

These three properties are all adorned with the fleur de lys. They were the former Science laboratory of the Grammar School, York House and Priory House respectively. The

latter became the new schoolhouse for the grammar school from 1835. The school was founded in 1561 in Becket's Chapel. It finally closed in 1903.

At the time Priory House was owned by Cornelius Tipple who exchanged it for Rook House in Vicar Street. In 1988 Tom Alderton who was living in York House which he had bought at auction, believed it had been used for grammar school boarders.

Priory House c. 1908

21-25 Middleton Street – Middleton's shop

This shop was once the property of His Honour, Judge Alpe. He was the Public Analyst and had a chemist's shop here which later moved across the road to where **Needlecraft** is now. Tom Turner, former Town Clerk has these memories:

' *His Honour Judge Alpe, lived in Bracondale, a house standing off the street opposite the war memorial. Bernard Stutely built his chalet on Alpe's former tennis court. Alpe had a garage attached to his house and an open yellow Vauxhall tourer, which nine times out of ten would never start! Arthur Pratt would give him a push and Billy Bales the roadman, would put his cart one side of the opening and his broom the other. Alpe's car would leap across Middleton Street and down Vicar Street and back again and he would lean out of his car and recognise the assistance of Billy Bales.'*

Alpe's chemist, now Middletons. This photo c.1885, pre-dates the war memorial & Town Hall. Billy Bales is in the road

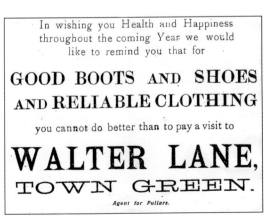

In wishing you Health and Happiness throughout the coming Year we would like to remind you that for

GOOD BOOTS AND SHOES AND RELIABLE CLOTHING

you cannot do better than to pay a visit to

WALTER LANE, TOWN GREEN.

Agent for Pullars.

Alpe's chemist later became Walter Lane, the Gentleman's Outfitters. In a room behind it George Reeve set up his own printing business in 1928. It later became Bedingfield's run by Muriel Bedingfield, as a drapery and clothes store. This later became Gilberts and is now Middletons.

Walter Lane outside his shop – note the Town Hall centre left

27, Middleton Street – Turret House

This house with its distinctive turret became a nurse's home in the First World War.

A game of croquet in progress in the garden behind Turret House in the early 1900s.

Anna Smith, Headmistress of Colwyn School, in Middleton Street, with some of her pupils outside Turret House

Mrs Knighton's memories of Turret House:

'At the nurses home there was Nurse Ada the matron and six nurses. I went to her for a nurse as I had ear ache and mother took me to young Dr. Hughes.
The nurses used to go out with doctors to patients and then the district nurses came in.'

Alpe's chemist

Our

Mrs Cora Knighton refers to Alpe's chemist's shop which moved across from where Middleton's is now and became J F Collin, famous for 'Collin's Bronchial Elixir' – the property is now Needlecraft.

Middleton Court
Mrs Knighton again:

'In this yard was **Colwyn School** *run by the sister of the butcher, Miss Peplum. The postman's daughter was one of the teachers, Miss Dye, also the stationmaster's daughter Miss Norman. I did not like nines. We wrote on slates. If I was given a sum with a 9 in it, I was allowed to rub it out and put what figures I wanted in. That was my first school - we had a Valentine's party and gave each other presents.'*

After Miss Norman married, the school was run by Miss Thornton, Miss France and Miss Nash. In 1912 Anna Smith took over and the school later moved across the road to Rook House in Vicar Street.

Pupils of Colwyn School, in Middleton Court, early 1920s

From about 1926 the **Roman Catholic Church** had its chapel in a school building in the courtyard. The first resident priest was Fr. T K Philips who stayed until 1934. Fr Ketterer took over and in 1938 the church moved to its present site in Norwich Road.

Priory Gardens
This attractive green area was the site of the gymnasium and Fives Court for the grammar school and where the new town Post Office was opened in 1940.

16, Middleton Street – now Rosedale Funeral Parlour
Next door to the Post office was once **Gipson's** green grocery. Before that it was one of the houses used for evacuees in 1939

Alice Pike, nee Keep – memories of an evacuee
'Our evacuation was arranged by a school in London off the Old Kent Road. I said a tearful goodbye to mother at Liverpool Street Station and six hours later we were at a country station I knew not where. The train stopped several times because of bombing.

The nine of us were tired and hungry and clutched our few belongings wrapped in brown paper tied with string. We were taken to a hall and then to an empty house next to the Post Office which we had to share with another family. The house is now Gipsons the green grocer (now Rosedale Funeral Parlour*). We were greeted by a lady* (WVS), *who gave us a box of rations and said we were in Wymondham, Norfolk.*

We had a bedroom upstairs, a living room downstairs and use of the kitchen.
After two weeks a lady who owned a shoe shop, said we could have her cottage which had been empty for years – it had three bedrooms, living room and kitchen but no electricity gas, water or toilet. But to us it was paradise. It was near Cavick House where the army was billeted. We got water in a bucket from the end cottage. Later the council installed a tap in the kitchen but we still had no sink. They emptied our bucket lavatory each week so now we didn't have to dig a hole in the garden and bury it ! We had paraffin lamps and candles and cooked on an open fire; breakfast was always porridge and dinner was stew – what else could you cook on an open fire ? Eventually we had a fire with oven installed.
We registered for food rations at Clarke's on Damgate Corner. Opposite was a baker's which sold meat patties at 4d which tasted like nectar. Some of us went to Browick School though Bob, who passed the 11 plus, went to a school in Norwich.'

Albert Boughen - another evacuee,
'I was 15 when I joined my family in Wymondham after bombs at Gravesend in mid 1940. We lived in various places - at Cavick Farm where there was no electric or water, Damgate, Silfield Avenue where the house used to be a fireman's and the bell went off at all hours and finally in Middleton Street, now Gipsons (now Rosedale Funeral Parlour).
As I had finished school I worked at the CWS brush factory and an oil pipe line before joining the Air Force. One day I was sitting

in a YMCA centre and another serviceman kept looking at me. It turned out that this man had lived opposite us (now Jarrold*) in Wymondham.'*

This property was used for evacuee families 1939-43

14 Middleton Street – Council Offices

Randall Burroughes had this property built 1794-5. He had inherited land from his father who died when he was six. By 1783 he was farming at Suton and Browick Hall and in 1790 he purchased all the other property in Wymondham which had belonged to his brother and uncle.

In 1992 he married Ann Denton, daughter of Jane and Samuel Denton of Burfield Hall. The marriage settlement brought him 202 acres. In return Randall built this house for his mother-in-law Jane Denton and paid her an annual allowance of £300.

By 1794 he had begun a farming diary which he kept until 1799. The diary has become a valuable historical document.

He moved to Burfield Hall in 1796 and Mrs Denton was in 14, Middleton Street, until 1809.

173

By the 1850s the house was occupied by John and Sarah Cann. In the 1880s Lionel Standley the auctioneer bought it and his family owned it until 1919 when it was sold for £1,200.

Mrs Kitty Hughes widow of Dr Maurice Hughes moved into the 'Ferneries' as it was then known, carrying on the practice using locums. Incidentally the wonderful slate slabs from the back garden, now adorn part of the courtyard at Wymondham Heritage Museum in the Bridewell. One of the locums Dr Roms bought it, then in 1920 John Rolfe a farmer became the owner.

The coach house at the back with its bell used to summon the doctor or his coachman, was used by the Heritage Society in the 1990s.

In 1938 Wymondham Urban District Council (UDC) bought the house and it acquired a smart Art Deco clock with their initials. When the UDC was dissolved in 1974 Wymondham Town Council was formed. In 1982 Wymondham Heritage Museum Association converted some outhouses at the rear, into a museum. The museum moved into the Bridewell in 1996.

8, Middleton Street – in the early 1900s, the premises of 'The Mallows' cab firm.

At the time of the photograph(1904) on page 174, Charles Mallows of Middleton Street, whose sign can just be seen to the right of the Town Council Offices, with cabs outside, had his cabs meeting trains at the station. Mallows also let rooms.

Market Street

3 Market Street, Parke's the butcher

This late 16th century building with its earliest section at the rear, now Peter Parke's butchers, was once a saddlers and harness maker's premises in the mid 19th century and has had a long history in the butcher's trade. The Cross family ran it for many years. During the Second World War, it was requisitioned by the Army and in 1946-7 it was acquired by Tom Parke. For a time he had a fish shop and dry cleaners there until he got his butcher's licence.

The photo c.1900s, shows Parke's before Tom Parke had the plaster removed to expose the wonderful timber beams.

Tubby Fulcher's memories of the butchery trade before fridges
'Jerry Cross was where Peter Parke is now. The meat was all on display. If it began to smell, they threw it away. Cross used to stand there with a fly swatter. They slaughtered out the back.'

Part of the timber framed rear of Parke's butchers, showing a mullioned window, in the earliest part of the property

11, Market Street – now Wymondham Pizzas & Kebabs
P Haldinstein & Son, the Boot & Shoe manufacturers, a Norwich firm, had a business in Wymondham with its workshop behind these premises.

15 & 17, Market Street – now the Little Computer Shop and the Health Shop
These two properties were once the premises of the Dog & Duck, a Cann & Clarke pub, where various members of the Cross family were licensees.

21, Market Street

This property was once occupied by Walter Little & Son, Gentlemen's Outfitters. The business had begun in Colegate Norwich in 1898. Other shops opened in St Benedict's and Magdalen Streets before the business expanded to Watton, Diss and Wymondham, where the sign over the shop included the slogan 'Lots are dressed by Littles'.

An advertisement dated 1932

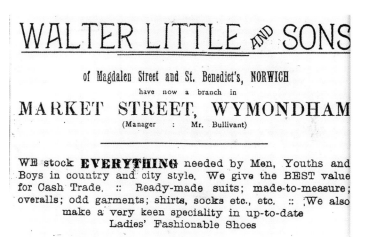

WALTER LITTLE AND SONS

of Magdalen Street and St. Benedict's, NORWICH

have now a branch in

MARKET STREET, WYMONDHAM

(Manager   :   Mr. Bullivant)

WE stock **EVERYTHING** needed by Men, Youths and Boys in country and city style. We give the BEST value for Cash Trade. :: Ready-made suits; made-to-measure; overalls; odd garments; shirts, socks etc., etc. :: We also make a very keen speciality in up-to-date Ladies' Fashionable Shoes

29, Market Street – the 'Heart of Wymondham,' formerly the 'White Hart'

For centuries this inn was known as the White Hart, one of the three most important inns in the town.

When the White Hart was renovated in 1973, scorched timbers, wattle and daub and clay features were uncovered indicating, that like so many Wymondham properties, there is an older core behind its 18th century façade.

In a Grisaugh Manor rental of 1526/7, a *'free messuage called the Harte, in the streete called Marketsteede'*, is listed next to *'the comon path called Welgate Lane'*. This lane was the path from Market Street to the present car park in Back Lane, under the archway next to the present 'Heart of Wymondham'. It is held in *'knightes service as appeareth by the handwriting of Richard Banyard gent'* ie. it was a small part of a medieval landowner's total acreage.

A mullioned window, on the original back wall of the White Hart, probably 16th century.

During the 1973 work the old Masonic room was discovered (seen here). It was made into a new restaurant.

At that time a three course lunch or dinner could be bought from £1. 00.

The central chimney is cut through from the front to the rear, forming an arched passage similar to Rook House in Vicar Street, rebuilt after the 1615 fire in the 1620s.

The archway entrance to the White Hart

In 1827 the White Hart advertised *'neat gigs with good horses and careful drivers'* In 1830 the Magnet coach was calling at 5.30pm at the White Hart en route from Norwich to London. By the mid 1830s three coaches of the Magnet company were running daily between Norwich and London, stopping at inns in Wymondham.

In 1919 Frank Cross's inventory of fixtures and fittings for the incoming tenant of the White Hart, Sidney Betts and Morgan's brewery, detailed *'a saddle room, bar, smoke room, top cellar, parlour, four bedrooms and a club room complete with two spittoons'*! All was lit by *'gas brackets fitted with incandescent burners'*

31-33, Market Street, Gazes, formerly Fred Standley & Sons, electricians

Ringer's Fish & Chip shop and the premises next door were pulled down and Standley's new electrical shop opened in 1965.

Before the demolition

And after !

Cottages behind Standleys

35-7, Market Street, Hemstocks jewellers, once the site of **Parker's Supply Stores**

Miss Lowe's memories of Parker's Supply Stores

The fire 1900

'Volunteer firemen would be paid so much an hour for 'pumping up'. They started firing maroons to call people up. I was terrified as it was next door to us. My grandfather was the honorary superintendent until his death.

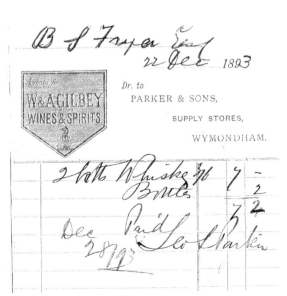

181

The last fire he put on a uniform for (1900), was at Parker's Supply Stores. It was a draper's, grocers, private house and show rooms and a very good dress maker. I was seven years old. Our house caught it a bit. In our hall stood a hand fire engine filled with water. This was trundled up the street and sprayed on our house and Barclays Bank.'

In this photo of the late 1890s, Parker's Stores can be seen, near right. After the fire of 1900, the present building now occupied by Hemstocks, was built. Miss Lowe's house, now the Consort Hotel, can be seen opposite Parkers.

Dry cleaning

'We sent dry cleaning to a firm in Perth because there were no local cleaners. The post was very efficient – three deliveries a day, a penny a letter and halfpenny a postcard. The parcel post was cheap. I think Parker's Supply stores were agents for

182

the cleaners. Shops were open 8am – 8pm with half a day on Wednesday.'

Market Place
1, Market Place
This property (near left in the next photo), was where Dr David Hughes had his practice. His son Dr Maurice Hughes, lived next door. He took over his father's practice at number 1, but in September 1914 he enlisted in the Army.

Dr Hughes is seen on the left in the next photo, before embarkation to the Dardanelles in 1915. He was killed in September 1915 and is buried in the 7th Field Ambulance cemetery.

Mrs Knighton's memories of Dr Hughes:
'I had ear ache as a child and mother took me to young Dr. Hughes. He decided I had tonsils and adenoid trouble. One morning two doctors arrived including young Dr. Hughes. Two nurses came from the nurses' home and went to mother's bedroom and stripped the

washstand and dressing table. Mother was told to have plenty of hot water. My tonsils and adenoids were taken out. The school doctor said it was the best he had ever seen done. The girls after me had hers at the Jenny Lind and there were bits left in. For four days I had just sips of hot water then a cup of tea.'

Dr Hughes on horseback on the left, shortly before embarkation

for Gallipoli

The Market Place & Market Cross

Wymondham was granted a charter for a three day annual fair by King Stephen in 1135 AD – this was renewed by Henry II. In 1204 King John issued the first known charter for a Friday market. Though the very first market in the town was near the Abbey, for centuries it has been on its present location. The shape and size of the market square has changed little since early times.

The first cross with simple shaft and stepped base dates from c. 1300 but it was the Elizabethan one like a small market hall with an upper chamber which was destroyed by the Fire of 1615. The design of the present cross is unusual – its creator obviously wanted to build something special. There are only two other market crosses in the country similar to it.

In this photo, possibly posed, c. 1890, the timbers of the Cross are blackened as was the fashion in Victorian times.

The Cross was used as a library for many years. Here are more books arriving in the 1930s.

In 1899 Ryder Haggard organised a 'universal bazaar' to raise money for this and to improve the library which was located there at the time.

The market cross has been restored on many occasions.

The King's Head Inn - now the Co-operative Food Store, 6 Market Place

The largest and most important inn in the town, the King's Head's prime position in the market place put it at the centre of trade. The photo below c.1912, shows the Georgian façade, but a 17th century letter written by Thomas Knyvett and left there for his wife, shows that the inn had a much longer history.

A hunt gathering in front of the King's Head c. 1912

The inn had its heyday during the golden age of coaching c. 1770s-1840s. Initially it was a staging post for horse drawn coaches like the London Post Coach and Norwich Mail. Later, coaches from the Telegraph Company stopped daily, en route between Norwich and London.

The coming of railways in the 1840s ended the prosperous age of coaching and with it, the most colourful period in the King's Head's history. However, the inn organised cabs to meet every train at Wymondham station for a fare of one shilling (see photograph of Wymondham station on page 123).

From the early 19th century, the inn was used as a courthouse dealing with lesser crimes. JPs met here in the Petty Sessions until the court moved to the Bridewell in 1879.

The King's Head was also an important social centre – many and various assemblies, concerts, balls and dinners were held in the spacious upper room. Auctions sales took place there and even included the sale of a windmill in 1794.

The coronations of George III and IV were celebrated there and the Wymondham Troop of Yeomanry Cavalry held their social functions at the inn.

In more recent times the inn had a bowling green and hosted committee meetings of the Wymondham Football and Cricket Clubs.

A view of the King's Head a few years before it closed in 1962

The King's Head Meadow had a long association with sports, celebrations, carnivals etc. The continuing presence of the town football club there is a reminder of the link between this popular green area and Wymondham's foremost inn which closed in 1962.

The inn was partly demolished and the site left derelict for some years. Eventually Woolworths acquired the land and opened there in 1981. Recently the Co-operative Food Store occupied the premises.

The former George & Dragon, 7 & 7A, Market Place – now
Nationwide Building Society & Ladbrookes

This photo taken by an American during the Second World War, shows the timbered front of the former George & Dragon, on the near left. It closed in 1928.
Tom Parke converted the left hand side of the building (just out of view), into a butcher's shop before moving to Market Street.
Charles Revells and P W Seppings continued to use the premises as a butcher's shop into the 1960s.

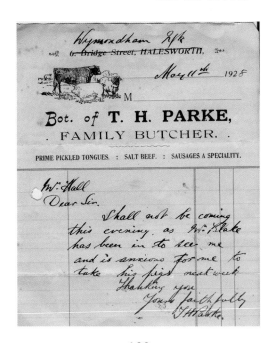

View of the 1935 carnival showing the King's Head and the former
George & Dragon next door

8, Market Place - now the Big 'C' Charity shop

Clements & Son once had
two shops in the town – in
Fairland Street and here.

This advertisement is dated
1898.

9 & 10, Market Place – now 'Chips Away' & the Norwich & Peterborough Building Society

The Wymondham Co-op opened in the town in 1891 moving to this prime position in the market place c. 1900. It is hard to imagine today how it could have made a profit selling groceries, meat, clothes and shoes when there were so many other shops in Wymondham selling the same products during this period. Every member had a Co-op number and the 'divi' was their share in the profits.

The Co-op with well stocked windows and smart staff, 1920s

It all ended in 1981 and now 'Chips Away' and the Norwich & Peterborough Building Society, trade in these premises.

11, Market Place – now in use as a veterinary practice.

This property was formerly the offices of Hall & Palmer, auctioneers, surveyors and estate agents. This company ran regular auctions on the site now occupied by the Wymondham Health Centre.

Bridewell Street – the road leading to the Bridewell

3, Bridewell Street

This property has an early 17th century casement and door case with a mullioned fanlight. In earlier times it was the butcher's shop of Kerridge and then Greene. The former shop had a drop down shutter forming the counter.

5 & 5A, Bridewell Street

In the 1970s these premises were remembered as Miss Bailey's bicycle shop but in 1914 Arthur Proctor had first set up his cobbler's business here. When he strarted he had £3. 00 to his name and some help from his parents. He sold boots and shoes and did repairs. Everything was hand sewn – he even made his own thread from six or seven strands of hemp.

191

In 1930 Arthur Proctor moved to the corner of Damgate and Church Street. George Reeve told him he would never succeed as shoppers always walked on the other side of the road! Proctor's shoe shop finally closed in 2012.

7 & 7A Bridewell Street

Frank Clarke opened his Ironmonger's shop here in 1912 in what seems to have been an off licence previously. Clive and Dennis Clarke in their brown shop coats were well known in the 1970s and 1980s.

Any problems in the DIY area could be solved by Clarke's or Clements'.

9, Bridewell Street,

This property was converted to residential use in the 1990s. One Sunday afternoon we had a call from the owner Mike Hayes who was renovating the house, asking us to come over.

He had taken up the floor pammets to reveal an earth floor with a slight depression in the centre of the room. He pointed out the burnt remnants of some old pieces of wood. Furthermore, the room had a distinct aroma of centuries old smoke with the floor up. Was this evidence of the Fire of 1615 ?

13 & 15 Bridewell Street

These houses still have their original jetties and most probably date from the early 17th century after the Fire of 1615.

17, 19, & 21 Bridewell Street

These properties have beams featuring the 'Wymondham school' mouldings. Number 21 was the Old Dairy Farmhouse which has a flint and brick cellar which could possibly be pre 1615, the year of the great fire. Number 19 was the buttery associated with the farmhouse.

Feature beam showing the 'Wymondham s c h o o l ' moulding

2, Bridewell Street - The Queen's Head

Robert Sadd, a blacksmith was referred to as the owner of the lands and tenements immediately west of the property known as the manor house. This was the Queen's Head site. Sadd died in 1563. His son John Sadd eventually inherited the premises and he died in 1583. The fire of 1615 destroyed the property and his descendant Robert Sadd's loss, was assessed at £220. The house was rebuilt and extended.

It is of boxed timber framed construction, jettied and with a cellar of flint and rubble walls under the eastern ground floor room. This could have survived from before the fire. The last Sadd to own the property was probably Christopher Sadd c. 1670.

John Barker a beer brewer owned the Queen's Head property from c.1690-1729. As was the custom he probably sold his beer on his own premises. By 1738 Thomas Barker was the owner. He let it to his son Thomas a worsted weaver. In 1755 his widow married John Grime Carter a wig maker of Wymondham who sold the inn to Diss Brewery. Carter became the land lord until 1810. During the early 1800s, Mack & Co's carriers en route from Norwich to London, called at the inn every day except Sundays.
The inn was with Diss Brewery until 1897 when it passed to Lacons and later Whitbread in 1965.

During the time when Thomas Rackham was the licensee from 1836-46, the frontage was bricked up and the jetty removed.

More recently Mrs Catherine Armstrong, whose son Michael has done so much to preserve the Regal cinema, became manageress and later licensee, 1969-73.

4, Bridewell Street - the Manor House

The appearance of this house suggests it dates from the 16th century although most of the houses in this side of the street were probably rebuilt after the fire of 1615. It has inscriptions on the beam above the fireplace – 'Live well and die never. Die well and live ever' and the name of an owner Richard Lincoln a wool merchant who owned the house from 1616-34. Over the front door there is a Latin inscription which means, 'My servant is not a dormouse, nor is the host a leech'.

When the house was up for sale in 1906, the auctioneer drew attention to it as 'one of the noted ancient houses of Wymondham, being built throughout with oak. It is in exceptionally good repair and well adapted for conversion to business purposes.' The sale details also revealed that it had a cart shed, granary and harness room and an enclosed yard with a good frontage to Bridewell Street. There was also a plentiful supply of good water and a right of way through the Queen's Head yard as a back entrance.

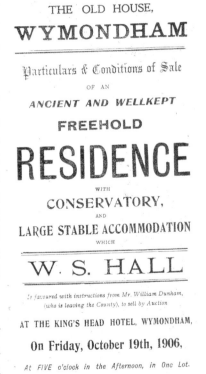

THE OLD HOUSE,

WYMONDHAM

Particulars & Conditions of Sale

OF AN

ANCIENT AND WELLKEPT

FREEHOLD

RESIDENCE

WITH

CONSERVATORY,

AND

LARGE STABLE ACCOMMODATION

WHICH

W. S. HALL

Is favoured with instructions from Mr. William Dunham, (who is leaving the County), to sell by Auction

AT THE KING'S HEAD HOTEL, WYMONDHAM,

On Friday, October 19th, 1906,

At FIVE o'clock in the Afternoon, in One Lot.

During the Second World War the house was furnished as a mother's club for evacuees with a playroom. Persuaded by Ethel Gooch the organiser of the WVS, the mothers helped to run the club from October 1940.

Bridewell Street, with the Manor House on left. This postcard was bought in Wymondham in 1944, by a doctor at the Morley hospital. He brought it back in the 1990s

Laying sewers down Bridewell Street, 1932 – the Bridewell can be seen in the background

12, Bridewell Street - Lyndhurst
For a time this property was used by Lyndhurst School whose main premises were at the Baptist Chapel in Brewery Lane.

14, Bridewell Street – a link with a 'Wymondham worthy'
For some years the late George Mabbutt lived here. About two years ago the present owner found an engraved silver presentation pencil from Briton Brush. George worked there for many years and the pencil was probably his. It is now on display in the Heritage Museum.

A mason's business in Bridewell Street

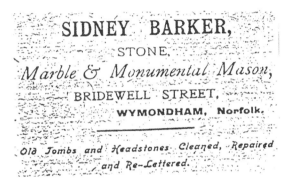

Also in this street were the shops and yard of the stone mason Sidney Barker.
It is uncertain as to which property this was. It was sold in 1927.

Back Lane

This lane was the boundary between the houses, outbuildings and yards of Market Street, Middleton Street and Town Green and the meadows, market garden (the Retreat nursery) and orchard to the north. Mrs Bedingfield in her memories said, *'Back Lane was quite narrow at one time and they called it Backside! Someone said I wish it was not called Back Lane and Tom Turner said well call it the old name then – Backside'.*
Originally however, it was called **Smallgate Lane**.

Off Back Lane is **Standley Court** named after the families who have served the town as electricians, vets, solicitors and antique dealers for many years.

Ogden Close got its name from Mr Ogden of Ogden's Chemist's shop on Market Street (now a charity shop).

R Plunkett & Sons

Robert Plunkett started out c. 1900 mending bicycles, but later he had a motor and general engineering business. Their forge was just off Bridewell Street and into Back Lane. Today it is the white house opposite Central Hall.

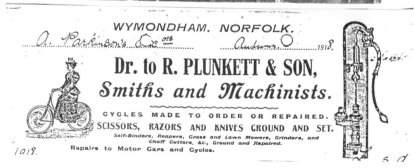

Photo c. 1905 - R. Plunkett kneeling. Advert dated 1918

Central Hall

This building was opened by Viscount Mackintosh of Halifax in December 1965. It cost just under £25,000 of which £10,000 was from a Ministry of Education grant. The remainder came from a variety of sources including money raised by the Victory Fund at the end of the Second World War. The hall has always been run by a volunteer management committee, which has recently completed a splendid refurbishment. It deserves the town's gratitude for providing a centre for many different activities for so many years. The land was given by Bullard's Brewery and was part of the old King's Head bowling green and meadow.

Norwich Road

Elm Terrace

On the 1826 plan of the **Bridewell Head Meadow** below, can be seen the Maltings of the Wymondham Brewery which were pulled down after 1894 and replaced by Elm Terrace.

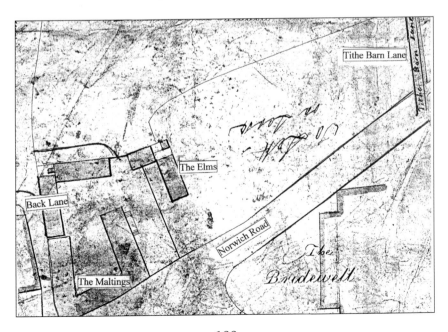

The Roman Catholic Church

Also shown on the plan is the Elms, which had belonged to the Clements family (ironmongers) for many years. The site was purchased by the RC Church in 1937 and the billiards room and stables were converted into the 'stable chapel'. In 1934 Father John Ketterer became priest and served mass to Roman Catholics in Wymondham and Attleborough as well as the airfields at Deopham and Hethel in wartime.

In 1946 Father Cowin became the priest. He had been chaplain to the 18th (East Anglian) Division and was taken prisoner with them in Singapore and became a prisoner of war in Changi.

A national appeal in 1948 for a church to be a permanent memorial to those who had lost their lives as Far East prisoners-of-war, enabled a church designed by Donovan Purcel to be built. A reredos was made by John Hester of Cambridge. Books inscribed with the names of 24,000 Far Eastern POWs who lost their lives are still being added to.

A large parish hall on the site was opened in 1995.

The church dedicated to the Blessed Virgin and St Thomas of Canterbury, was extended in 2001. This was designed by Wymondham architect Paul Lucas. It was awarded the South Norfolk Design Award.

Orchard Way – built on the site of a former orchard and meadow Another name on the plan is **Tithe Barn Lane**, later known as **Windmill Lane**. The late Marian Roberts, a museum steward, came to live in Orchard way in 2002 and wanted to know why it was so called. This is what she wrote about her discovery:

'I learnt that it had been a big meadow and that apples from the orchard there were purchased by Gaymers of Attleborough, famous for its cider.

I know the development began in the late 1960s with 15 houses in a cul-de-sac from Norwich Road. It was later extended in the manner we see today. According to the original brochure of the 'Tithe Barn Estate', Hackett's Builders appear to have been replaced by Norfolk Garden Estates Ltd. The architects were Chaplin & Farrant and the main contractors Thetford Construction Ltd. The agents were Knight Benjamin & Co, 43, All Saints Green, Norwich.'

These new houses were marketed as **Tithe Barn Estate,**

The Tithe Barn

Originally there were two Tithe Barns. The Abbey Barn which was part of the monastery founded in 1107 received the tithes – a tenth part of the gross produce of the soil paid annually by parishioners to support the church or clergy.

When the monastery was pulled down, the barn remained and the tithe rights were leased out to lay people who shared them with vicars. This barn seems to have lasted until the early 19th century.

Enter the Baileys

By the 1830s the Bailey family who had the lease of the Abbey barn also owned the other Tithe Barn which was reached by a lane called Windmill Lane next to the Windmill pub in Norwich Road. In 1839 yearly payments for tithe were £2,169.16s 6d to Thomas Bailey and £772 3s 8d to the vicar, which were very large sums. The Horner family inherited from Thomas Bailey.

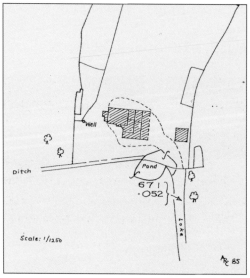

A sketch map of the tithe barn by Tony Cartwright

New owners and a new life

In 1921 Charles Robert Ayton bought 'Tithe Barn'. It was then sold on to Wallace W Poll in 1934. It had many uses until it was sold to Hacketts' Builders in 1963. Chickens and animals were kept on the land nearby. Mr Standley kept antiques he had bought at Hall & Palmers sale there. Gymkhanas were held there in the 1940s. In the post-war housing shortages, several young married couples had caravans down there. A donkey called 'Jerusalem' lived in the orchard!

Memories;

Mr Philip Bunn and his wife lived in one of the caravans from 1958-63. They bought the first dwelling to be built in Rothbury Road in 1969 for £2,990. Hacketts began building in Rothbury Road from the Pople Street end and later Norfolk Garden Estates took over the development.

Mr John Fulcher

I lived down the Old Tithe Barn with Granny in the little bungalow. There was a garden, shed and the big barn. Aytons' kept horses and a tumbrel down there to use in the gravel pits. Granny's second husband loaded up the stone for Aytons'. It was then taken to the little siding at the station and put into open trucks. Later it was used on the roads.'

After they gave up using horses, Dairy Crest kept milk floats down there. The Avenue garage site was also stables. Tithe Barn has gone and is now Orchard Way.

The Windmill public house

This is said to be an early coaching inn dating from the 15th century. Its location at the entrance of the town certainly makes it a convenient stopping place for coaches.

Early records say that Thomas Randall the Wymondham brewer, in 1738 gave to Thomas Randall his grandson, a tenement called 'the Windmill Sails' whose occupier was John Brown. The pub was still so named in a conveyance of 1876. The earliest recorded licensee was John Miller, 1822.

Choseley Court

This road was named after the manor of Choseley. The subject of Wymondham manors is very complex. Mr Pomeroy explains Choseley manor as follows:
'This manor was given by William d'Albini to God and St Mary and the church of St Lazarus of Jerusalem at Burton and the bretheren serving God there for the souls of King Stephen and Maude his Queen. He also founded Westwade Chapel where the church of St Lazarus had a master and two bretheren there to get alms from those who passed by.'

After the dissolution 1538, Henry VIII gave it to John Dudley In 1545 he sold it to William Kett. But after Kett's Rebellion, 1549, it was confiscated. John Dudley was now the earl of Warwick, ironically the man who led the army which crushed Kett's rebel force at Dussindale.
It was in time restored to Kett's descendants but eventually it was sold to the Great Hospital in Norwich.

Wymondham Academy High School

The land on which the school stands was owned by Charles Ayton. It had been a football ground and showground. When he died he left it to the town and it was sold to Norfolk County Council for a school to be built on the site.

Initially known as a senior school, it became a secondary modern, then a high school, before its current status as Wymondham Academy High. Built in 1938-9 to accommodate 300 pupils it had an assembly hall and stage, gymnasium, craft workshops domestic science rooms and large playing fields. As a result of raising the school leaving age to 15 in 1946, the pupil numbers soon rose to 400.

NORFOLK COUNTY COUNCIL
EDUCATION COMMITTEE

Official Opening

OF

WYMONDHAM SENIOR SCHOOL

BY

Sir Frederick Mander, M.A., B.Sc.

General Secretary, National Union of Teachers

MONDAY, 8th MAY

1939 - at 2.30 p.m.

The High School in the Second World War

In September 1939 a 1,000 or so evacuees arrived from Gravesend. The High School was the main reception centre and they were given

204

refreshments and taken to their new hones.
Pat Gittings an evacuee, remembers the occasion:
'At Wymondhmam High School we waited for people to choose us and it was awful standing there with a label round our necks'

Air raids
When there were air raids the rule was, if you could not get home under 5 minutes from hearing the siren, you stayed at the school. The cloakrooms and changing rooms had their walls reinforced and the windows were shuttered for the protection of the children.
Air raids were frequent in 1940 and the school log book records that in the two weeks ending 6 Dec 1940, 878 child hours out of 11,376, were interrupted by air raids ie 7.7 %.

The roof of the High School was earmarked by the local Home Guard commander, who planned to use it as a suitable site for a defensive position in the event of an invasion.
Incidentally the school's Headmaster Mr Purchase was the first Wymondham man to enrol in the Local Defence Volunteers (LDVs), on 14 May 1940. A few months later the organisation, was renamed the Home Guard.

Margaret Reeve Close
This cul-de-sac was named after a former head teacher at what is now Wymondham Academy High, Mrs Margaret Reeve.

The housing development here was built on the site of the former **Wymondham Laundry** which started business in the 1890s in Cock Street. A new laundry was opened on this site in 1913 and finally closed in 1969.

Wymondham's first superstore Pricerite, was built on the site soon after 1971.

A group of laundry workers at the Cock Street works before the laundry moved to Norwich Road

89, Norwich Road

Between 1939 and 1944 there were 1,527 air raid warnings in Wymondham. On 5 January 1941 this house was the unlikely target for a machine gunner when the garage roof was hit by bullets and a pair of boot were damaged !

At the time this house was the home of Eva & George Chapman.

Memories of Eva Chapman

'When war broke out on a Sunday in 1939, my husband went to Yarmouth to make final arrangements for the evacuees. He asked if I would use the car to take the evacuees to Spooner Row, Silfield and Suton.

People did not mind children but not women and children. They came by boat to Yarmouth and stayed the night at the race course or schools – they were tired and grubby.

I used to get houses ready for evacuees – I asked for donations of curtains, blankets etc and I scrubbed floors. My husband looked out for two little girls for me aged 10 and 11.   I had left my own little

boy next door. (In the end however, Mrs Chapman had Betty Hoiles and her sister Jean and a brother went next door) *They all became part of our family. Betty and Jean loved Philip, aged four.*
A lot of children did not settle and there was nothing for them to do. The only open space was Fairland Green. Their teachers came with them and they stayed a year or so until the bombing at Gravesend stopped.
When the siren went my husband would go to the Fire Station. As they passed my house on the Norwich road they would ring their bell to let me know they were going to Norwich. It was day and night work. Sometimes we did not hear the ALL CLEAR. My brother-in-law was in the Home Guard and he would knock on the windows and say 'the All Clear went an hour ago'.

Norwich Common – a distinct community

The memories of Mrs Fulcher, a long term resident there reveal much of what life was like on the common in the late 19th and early 20th centuries.
Mrs Fulcher:
'In those days there was the pub, 'The Old Oak' (listed in Harrods directory of 1868 and now a private house), the school, now part of the garage and St Edmunds Church, the Mission Hall, now a day nursery.
The school was built in 1849 by the National Society, for 40 children with two teachers with a mistress in charge. We had to walk to Wymondham for cookery lessons. We started school at 9 o'clock until 12 and came back at 1.30 to 3.30. We had a month to six weeks for harvest'.

By 1888 the school described as Board Common (mixed), had an average attendance of 16 boys and 27 girls. In 1896 it was for 80 children, average attendance being 58 and the mistress was Miss

Kate Mann who was still there in 1912 with 72 children and an attendance of 63. The school closed in 1935.

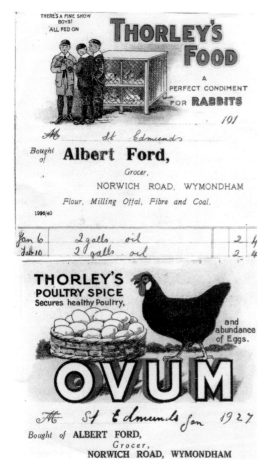

There was also a shop run by the Ford family.

The Kelly's directory for 1888 lists George Ford shopkeeper (common) and in 1912 Ann Ford (Mrs) shopkeeper, Norwich Road.
By 1925 it was Albert Ford, shopkeeper.

By the 1970s the shop had closed.

On a map of Norwich Common in 1890, can be seen the church, school and the pub, also a mill yard. Here there was a post mill in which all the machinery revolved on a massive post.
Mrs Fulcher continues:
'The Wymondham children did not like us 'commoners' and called us 'the common kids'. One girl pulled me off my bike when I tried to go 'up town'. She told me I could not go up there. We did not

mix and get to know each other. There were lots of children on the common then but only about half a dozen now (1980s). There were more houses then, several have been pulled down including one row of seven which was flooded out in 1912.'

Kett's Oak c. 1890 (above), showing the split in the trunk and in the 1930s, with railings and a cement filling.

'There were some houses down the lane to the railway – a lot of children came from there. We would go for walks and stand for hours by the railway crossing gate and watch the trains go by. We were told not to go through and we never did. The doctor had to borrow a bicycle to see patients down that lane !'

'There was a big house down the drive by the lodge (Downham) *and we went at 6 o'clock for our milk. It was 4 pints a penny for skimmed and they made lovely butter.*
I had a lovely childhood. I liked my teachers but not history. When I was a child we had a horse and cart. After harvest, dad used to take us for half a day to Yarmouth by train from Wymondham. I had a lovely mother and father and a happy life but I was born in an age when we took things quietly. We went to Sunday school and church at the St Edmund's Mission church ((built 1892) because the Wymondham kids didn't like us. We had 'treats'- the choir outing was at Browick and the Sunday school one at Stanfield or Kimberley. They took us in a tumbrel and there were swings there.'

St Edmund's Mission Church, Norwich Common

'Nearly all children went to Sunday school and we looked forward to it in those days. We had a Bible class at church but then we went to a private house when we were about 18. Mrs Pomeroy (Vicar Street*), took a class of about 10 of us. That was how the two of us* (Mr Fulcher and I) *met.*

210

'Father was a farm labourer and I sometimes walked to work with him. On Good Friday – at about 10 am 7 or 8 of us would walk to Hethersett, look at the church and gather violets and primroses. We were back by 4pm.

Mrs Fulcher's first job

' One day my sister who was in service came home and asked if I would like to live with her. I was only 14 and we cycled 18 miles there. She kept telling me it was just round the corner, but it took two and half hours. So I went into service. It was service or the factory then. There were four of us sisters there. I got on well and worked myself up and got married from there. I could get out from there when I shouldn't have done if you know what I mean ! My sisters would cover for me when I was courting. It was very nice there.'

Mrs Smith b. 1890

'I went to school up on Norwich Common near the Old Oak pub. My father worked at Browick Hall with the dairy herd. There were five of us and we used to get in the old oak tree (Kett's Oak*) when we were kids.*

We were very hard up. People going by in charabancs when we were playing out used to throw coins at us. There was a little shop up there facing the school run by Mr Ford – the 'sack' man's father. Mother had nothing - if we asked for another round of bread we could not have it. There is another day tomorrow she used to say. After school we went 'sticking' to get wood for the fire. I left school at 13 and went into service'

Tom Turner's memories – he became the Town Clerk

' In 1945 I bought a plot, a one acre barley field belonging to Jack Barnard of Elm Farm, Norwich Common on Norwich Road. Because it was wartime you could not build more than 1200 square feet and there was a spending limit. Outbuildings had to follow when restrictions were lifted.

211

Number 145, Norwich Road was already built by Mr Hovell, engineer at Briton Brush. The design won him a prize in one of the national newspapers for cost effectiveness.'

Probably a familiar site for the Norwich Common community. Trader Sam Marshall, seen here by Kett's Oak c. 1912

Hart's Farm Road – see under Hart's Farm Estate below

Kett's Park

The road and the park are named after Wymondham's most famous son Robert Kett, leader of the Norfolk rising 1549. Young oak trees grown from acorns obtained form Kett's Oak, were planted here by pupils of Robert Kett School in 1999 to commemorate the 450th anniversary of Kett's Rebellion.

Moot or Mote Hill – also known as Grisaugh or Gristlewood

The plan of the site shows how near it is to the railway and the A 11.

This ancient site can be seen from Kett's Park. The latest thinking is that it was a short lived 12th century Norman castle – an earth mound with timber ramparts. But William d' Albini, lord of the manor, decided he preferred to live at Old Buckenham where he built another castle. A gold ring dated 1306, belonging to Katherine Bigot, wife of Roger Fitz-Ortet of Stanfield Manor, was found on this site.

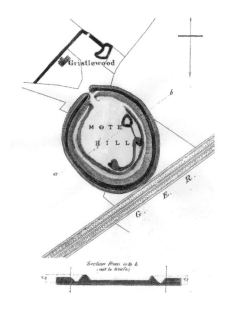

View of a rampart & ditch at Moot Hill

Hart's Farm Estate

This is named after a Mr Hart and a sketch map of Wymondham in the 1790s shows Mr Hart as occupier of the farm fronting on the common about one kilometre west/north west of Browick Hall.

In 1995 an archaeological field survey of the farm, found 291 pieces of medieval domestic pottery dating from 11th – 15th centuries. Hart's Farm house is a high quality early 17th century timber framed house, remodelled in the 18th century with a new wing added. This may have been used for weaving.

Memories of Tom Alderton, an agricultural labourer

''I left school at 14 on a Friday and started work on Monday at Grove Farm on Tuttles Lane. I carted straw for bullocks for Hubert Redding. I left and went threshing and when that stopped and I had no money I had to have a means test and went in front of the Board of Governors at the Wicklewood Workhouse. They asked me questions about my family.

When I left I worked for Mr Sheldrake at Harts Farm. I hand milked 18 cows twice a day beginning at 6.30am. I had a day off a fortnight. Then they got a milking parlour and a tank to cool milk.'

Norwich Road again
54B Wymondham Dell

Charles Robert Ayton had many interests in this road. He had land where Wymondham Dell Bowls Club is now. It was quarried at first and he later opened a second gravel pit near Semmences'. Mrs Cyril Ayton remembers the Dell site:

'He let Cyril (his son) *have it and he brought Cumberland turf to Norfolk for the first time for the bowling greens. Lesley Barnard was also involved.'*

The pit was filled in and by 1937 it had become Wymondham Dell Bowling Club. Later Lesley Barnard opened the Dell café on the site.

In the First World War, Capt Malcolm Ayton was awarded the MC and the **Vimy Ridge** houses were named in his honour.

Mr Wilson's memories of Vimy Ridge:

'I worked at Kiddle and Smallwood, a wood turning factory situated in Vimy Ridge. They made short brush handles and broom heads and various other things eg. chair and table legs turned on the lathes powered by a large engine that drove the shafting through the factory.

Mr Kiddle and his son ran the factory assisted by a few other workers. They made cylindrical broom heads sawn in half and drilled ready to be filled with stiff bass bristles. They were then taken to Mr Carter's of Pople Street where the bristles were inserted in the brushes. Then they were painted and polished ready for sale.'

The Women's Institute Hall (WI)

On the corner of Vimy Ridge and Norwich Road was the home of the Wymondham WI formed in 1920. In 1939 it was taken over by the military and on land adjoining, were three tents and a field kitchen. Before the arrival of 1,000 evacuees in the town on 3rd September1939, the hall had been open each day for clothing and blankets to be donated for the evacuees.

In 1965, when Central Hall opened, the WI Hall was put up for sale, demolished and new houses were built on the site.

76, Norwich Road – formerly Rydal Mount

In 1914 when Edwin Gooch married Ethel Banham they had a house built here called Rydal Mount opposite the WI Hall. Its name today is Quedem House.

34, Norwich Road – formerly Semmence

Semmence coach building and motor works moved to Norwich Road from Poynt House in Chapel Lane c.1918. This site had been their timber yard. The business then developed as carriers of sugar beet, and timber for the brush works.

Messrs Hall Palmer. (camp) 193?

Dr. to **H Semmence & Co** (H.L.SEMMENCE)

Wymondham Norfolk

TEL. No. 35

MOTOR AND AGRICULTURAL ENGINEERS, CARTAGE CONTRACTORS
CHAR-A-BANC PROPRIETORS AND FORD SERVICE AGENTS
STAND No. 98—NORWICH CORN HALL

In the Second World War, the army took over part of the premises for a field bakery to supply camps and bases around Norwich. Gordon Semmence continued the goods and passenger carrying service after the war. Gradually the coach business became permanent. We used to enjoy spotting Semmence's coaches around the country and many school outings were enjoyed from Morley School with Tim Semmence.

View of Semmence's garage and other buildings behind

Kimberley Street

Sir John Wodehouse, 1st Earl of Kimberley (1826-1902) of Kimberley Hall, was a prominent Victorian politician who served in all Gladstone's Liberal governments. A date plaque 1905, suggests this road was named after him.

There are no signs now of the brick works which were behind the Bridewell which existed from the late 18th century until 1900.

Guides & Scouts Headquarters

In September 1975 a new headquarters was officially opened. At that time it was used by over 300 scouts and guides every day of the week. It cost £14,000 (at the time a detached dwelling in Hubbard Close cost £9,000). The money was raised over 14 years. Mr Thompson became scout leader and and asked to join the project initiated by Dolly Attewell Captain of the 2nd Wymondham Guides. He dealt with financial matters.

The land behind one of the houses in this street was bought for just £750. Gordon and Tim Semmence helped with access across their land and Paul Hawkins built the headquarters on a non-profit making basis.

Memories of Dolly Attewell

'I joined the Guides in 1920s but had to hide my uniform because my family didn't think it was right to join the Association. I was mischievous and played up Captain Anna Smith of the 1st Wymondham Guides, who turned me out. I rejoined a year later and in 1930 became lieutenant of the 2nd Wymondham Guides.'

In 1976 to mark her great contribution, Dolly was presented with a garden seat and bouquet from members of the Wymondham community as well as the Guides.

Norwich Road - The Bridewell or House of Correction

Wymondham's first Bridewell is mentioned in 1619 in the Town Book. Its purpose was to deal with offences such as vagrancy, disorder and theft. A basement of a medieval merchant's house just behind the present building was used as a dungeon. Here prisoners were kept in chains in darkness.

The present building dating from 1785, resulted from a visit to the first Bridewell by John Howard who condemned it as *'vile, with sickly inmates'.*

Sir Thomas Beevor of Hethel Hall led a group of JPs in drawing up rules and a design for a new prison. Based on the reforming ideas of Howard it would be *'a seminary of industry and reformation instead of a receptacle of idleness and corruption'.* The discipline was firm but not harsh though hard labour was applied where appropriate. However the main aim was to treat the prisoners humanely, keep them usefully employed and reasonably fed.

Prisoners had a clean shirt each week and clean straw but they had to clean their rooms daily.

Part of the Bridewell in Norwich Road. On the left, the maltings c. 1880-90. They were demolished in 1894

The Norfolk Chronicle makes frequent reference to the Bridewell. For example, in 1785 *'John Turner and Ben Cuninngham weaver and husbandman, stole 2 geese, one chicken and a fat pig'* and were committed to the Bridewell.

Sometimes a prisoner was transferred for transportation to Australia. One such woman was the redoubtable Elizabeth Pulley whose record is well documented. On three occasions 1779-81 she stole clothes, goods or money. She spent 3 weeks in the Bridewell and was publicly whipped in the town. But she offended again and was given 12 months hard labour. In 1782 she stole cheese, bacon, butter, flour and other items from a Hethersett shop. She was sentenced to hang but this was commuted to transportation. Eventually she was put on a convict ship in 1787.
She later married Anthony Rope, another prisoner. They had seven children and 38 grandchildren.

In 2008 a great, great…. granddaughter visited the museum which tells her story.

In 1837 a prison inspector reported that a 14 year old girl had been sentenced to transportation for setting fire to hay stacks.

An advert in the Norfolk Chronicle 1843

Wymondham House of Correction
FEMALE TURNKEY WANTED.

WANTED IMMEDIATELY,
For the House of Correction at Wymondham,

A FEMALE TURNKEY to assist the Matron in the duties of the Prison. She must not be less than 35 years of age, be able to read and write, and produce unexceptionable testimonials of her ability for the situation. A widow without incumbrance, will be preferred.

Application to be made to Mrs. Johnson, the Matron of the Prison.

What came to be called a 'new model' prison, opened in 1785 with cells for 15 men and 6 women. Ten more cells were added later. Many counties wrote to Beevor for details of the plan of the Wymondham Bridewell, its rules and diet etc. A house for the prison governor, the present façade, was added in 1810.

The Bridewell in the 1930s

In 1788 the Norfolk Chronicle reported that *'Andrew Beck and Richard Day were committed to the Bridewell for three months for dragging nets in the nightime for birds.'* There are several references to prisoners being given *'hard labour for idle and disorderly behaviour'.*

However, Howard would have been pleased with a prisoner who *'was in 1795 discharged* (after two years*) as he'd made himself a master of the trade of hickling or combing tow with great diligence and had earned 10/- a wk. He was given £4.19s 6d for work he had done while an inmate.'*

In 1828 the prison closed but reopened as the County gaol for women in 1832. Inmates did all the laundry for male prisoners at Norwich gaol. The census records for 1841-71 show that there were some 20-23 women inmates including six or seven listed as 'lewd' women amongst them and several infants under one - presumably children of the prisoners. The main offences were stealing clothes, cloth or money. Inmates would shout abuse from their cell windows overlooking Norwich Road.

This view of the Bridewell has the words 'Police Station' on the far right of the building

Wymondham Bridewell has also served as a **police station** 1850- 1963, and a **courthouse** 1879-1991. When the court closed the building became derelict until rescued by Wynondham Heritage Society. With the aid of grants, it was renovated for a multi-purpose new role.

Browick Road – the road to Browick

2 & 4, Browick Road
These houses (centre right in the photo), were designed as a meeting house for the Plymouth Bretheren by the architect Thomas Jeckyll, born in Wymondham in 1827. The distinctive mouldings of flowers and fruit can still be seen under the eaves.

10, Browick Road – Browick Road Infant School

In 1872 the Wymondham School Board was set up and Wymondham Board School was built in 1876 for 180 boys, 180 girls and 200 infants at a cost of £5,886, with accommodation for a master and caretaker.
In 1896 a junior mixed department for 120 pupils was added.

Corston's mineral water factory chimney can be seen centre.

Wymondham Board School c. 1900

Staff in 1888: Mr RC Shockley master, Miss Jessie Mann, mistress, Miss Anne Burbage, infants.

A Browick Board School group photo c. 1895-6 - Tom Wharton is being held by the teacher top left, Edwin Gooch is 3rd left, 2nd row from top.

Extracts from School Log Book:

1882 Jan 26 - all children living on the 'Lizor' Lizard to be sent home owing to a case of smallpox in the district
1895 Oct 10 - Punished ....for going home without leave at playtime. The father came at night and challenged me to come out on the road and fight
1898 Nov 15 - Children let out of school a little earlier as there is a menagerie in town.
1905 Mar 1 – W Bowden, late scholar, has obtained a 1st class honours at Cambridge
1915 Oct 8 - Sgt Barnard visited the school and drilled the boys
Ethel Gooch taught here from 1914 and was Head Teacher of the Junior School from 1918-23.

The top class at Browick Road Junior School on Coronation Day 1953,
Back row l to r: G Bedingfield, A Sidell, H Patrick, P Nicholls, S Spinks, P Larke, J Garrod **Mid row l to r:** J Dack, P Braid, S Cowles, J Holmes, E Youngs, R Dodman, J Ebbage, J Ryder, M Metcalf, A Jackson, J Fisher, A Hewitt, A Cleaver, R Bartram, P Reeve, W Bateman, B Snelling
Front row l to r: J Cole, P Blythe, P Smith, V Blake, K Lain, M Hemmings, T Hearn, B Chamberlain

Some memories of life at Browick School

Tubby Fulcher b. 1906
'Jimmy Sparkes was the schoolmaster. He had some 'clever guys' who thought they could run the school. He tamed them. They say that punishment is not a deterrent but if you went to JS, you made sure you did not go again! If you did not learn in school hours he was prepared to stay after school and make sure you did'.

Tom Alderton
'I was born in Fairland Street and went to Browick School with Mr Sparkes, Miss King and Mrs Ethel Gooch. Mr Sparkes used to cane us. If you were a poor boy you copped it. The upper classes did not have it as bad. We sometimes had lessons outside and took our own lunch. I left school at 14 on Friday and started work on Monday on Tuttles Lane'.

Miss Lowe b. 1893, daughter of Dr Lowe
'I had two governesses and then went to school in Norwich but I remember Browick School. The first building was the headmaster's house, then the boys school, then the girls and then the mistress'

225

house. One did not live there but the school attendance officer did. He was known as 'The Kidhunter.'

Mrs Cora Knighton, b 1898

'My first school was a run by Miss Peplum who got married to the vet and gave it up. I then went to what we called 'Browick College' the only state school in Wymondham then. I remember the 'Kidhunter' as we called him, living at the school. He hunted up kids absent from school'.

School attendance was made compulsory for 5-10 year olds in 1880 and in 1918 for all children to the end of term in which they reached 14.)

Gladys White b 1899

'I lived down Frogshall and my father worked at Semmence's wood turnery. I was the youngest of four girls and went to Browick School from 3 -13. I took the Labour exam to leave school to start work. I passed and went to work at Bungard's shop (now Hemstocks*). I served there - the biggest place in town'.*

This photo and the previous one, show Browick Board School girls being prepared to be mothers or maids !

Browick School staff in 1979

14, Browick Road – now Windmill House Care Home

Corston's mineral water factory was located here. It closed in 1977

16, Browick Road – formerly Browick Mill

This mill was built in 1833 to replace an earlier post mill. In 1845 Wiliam Jermyn was miller but this mill had its heyday from 1864 when Jethro Littlewood Jarrett ran it. By 1888 it was described as 'operated by wind and steam'. At this time it was a **smock mill** – a wooden tower with six to 12 sides mounted on a brick base. In 1912 Henry Bird & Son corn dealers of Middleton Street, operated the mill.

Memories of Pauline Brown b. 1904:
' The Bird family were millers at Browick smock mill and had a shop in Market Street until at least 1918. My mother-in-law remembered

227

her father getting up in the night to reset the windmill sails. She also recalled going straight from Browick Road school back to the shop to weigh corn, yeast etc for the customers. On the way to school she would call in at the bakers' with the uncooked bread and return for it on the way home'

In 1925 the sails were blown off in a gale and it was eventually demolished. The mill house which was in the grounds, still stands. Incidentally the windmill may be remembered in the name **Post Mill Close.**

Browick Road Recreation Ground – formerly one of Ayton's stone pits.

The next photo shows stone pickers at work in Browick Road. Ayton employed some 200 men at one time.
The gravel pits

Charles Ayton's business began with five men and two carts and involved digging good quality gravel from local pits in Wymondham, which was then used for road making. His pits

were at Silfield, Strayground and Browick (now the Recreation Ground).
He also bought land where the Wymondham Dell Bowling Club is now which was quarried at first. He then opened a second pit near Semmence's.

Wymondham Rifle Club used to meet in the gravel pits. This photo is dated 1914. The father of Ethel Gooch Charles Banham is 2nd left middle row.

Work begins on the Recreation Ground
In 1933 when Edwin Gooch was chairman of the parish council, plans for the new Browick Recreation Ground began

Edwin Gooch centre, with long coat and trilby, with other councillors watching the start of work on the Rec.

Browick Road Council Houses
The first ten such houses were completed in 1922, with six more following in 1925-6. They can be seen in the background of the previous photo.

Gunton Road
Twenty two houses in this road were completed in 1926. The road may have got its name from Gunton's the Costessey Brickmakers.

Ayton Road – named after the Ayton family
In 1958 Ayton Asphalte became a member of the **May Gurney** group with its works on the corner of Ayton and Browick Roads. It remains a specialist manufacturer in bituminous materials and products for the building and civil engineering industries.
Before Aytons, **Henry King** had his furniture business on the site.

Memories of Dick Hewitt b. 1908
'My *father worked for Mr King the timber merchant- old Mr King. He had a furniture factory at Browick and my father worked there on a big saw cutting planks from trees. All King's men went on strike but not father. He never joined a union. They wanted more money and all stood outside the gateway. Then it all died down.*
One day the hunt were after a deer and it came in and cowered in the corner of the sawmill'

Browick

Browick Road leads to a fascinating and historically important part of the parish of Wymondham – the small community marked 'Brathwayte' on Faden's map of 1797 and 'Browick' on the first Ordnance Survey map c. 1850. 'Thwaite' is a Viking word for a village in a clearing.

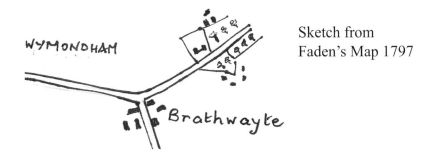

WYMONDHAM

Sketch from
Faden's Map 1797

Brathwayte

Sketch from Ordnance
Survey Map 1850

WYMONDHAM   Browick Hall

Browick

Browick Hall

At the centre of this small community is this hall. Randall Borroughs (1761-1817), whose name is remembered in **Burroughs Way**, farmed here from 1783-99 at least. The hall dates from the 17th century with 18th century additions. He later moved to Burfield Hall and farmed there too. He had married Anne Denton, daughter of Samuel Denton of Burfield.

Randall Burroughs' farming journal

He kept a farming journal which was very unusual and even made his own ink. He was a well respected JP and Deputy Lieutenant, a trustee of the Buckenham turnpike and member of the Great Yarmouth Pier and Haven Commission. His farming system integrated animal and arable husbandry. Arthur Young mentioned him in his Annals of Agriculture 1804.

His farming system

The basic Norfolk crop rotation was wheat, barley, turnips, and clover or grasses. But he did not adhere strictly to this. Turnips were eaten off the fields by sheep and carted to the cattle in the yard. He used horses for carting, ploughing, harvesting and coaching. In 1778-9 he had 160 sheep, a few pigs and geese and pigeon nesting boxes. His cattle were sold to Mr King the local butcher, at Norwich market or taken to Tasburgh to meet the drovers who took one week to take them to Smithfield.

His workers

Norfolk men worked hard for low wages. In 1795 Taylor got 7/- a week plus house rent and Kiddle 7/- plus a cottage and fuel. By 1799 most workers were employed by the day – piece work

Harvesting & haymaking

In 1795 ten men and one boy received 8/- an acre in payment. They were given 12 bottles of porter followed by a 'frolic' with half a leg of beef. In 1796 seventeen wagons were filled at haymaking and the women and boys who helped, got 7 pence a day but no beer!

The Fryer family

By 1886 the Fryer family were living at the hall, but there was a disastrous fire and much was destroyed. During World War Two, Major Fryer was CO of the local Home Guard. Several Land Girls worked at Browick Hall farm.

Land Girls remember
Mrs Cavill, nee Wicks

'I joined at 17 and knew Mr Fryer needed help as my father worked for him. My sister Peggy was also a Land Girl and we worked on the milk round. We were taught how to march for a special parade through the town.'

Mrs R Smith

'I was a Land Girl for Mr Fryer at Browick Hall. We delivered milk in all weathers even on Christmas Day. In the summer we worked in the cornfields weeding.

There were nine girls working on the farm but only one from 'away.' Audrey Townsend had a horse (Molly) and cart. She washed and rinsed the milk bottles and we all helped fill them and put on the foil tops.

The milk round was a very big one. We started at 7am and used a grey Ford van. One day a wheel came off at the bottom of Melton Hill. Another time it wouldn't start and we had to take a cart horse and tumbrel. The bottles rattled and scared the horse, which ran off. We just managed to stop before the Browick Road railway crossing which was shut!

We delivered milk to an underground secret post on Tuttles Lane. One day we looked down the steps and the door opened and a man told us that we weren't supposed to be there.

They were the happiest days of my life!'

A group of Land Girls at Browick Hall Farm, on Christmas Day 1945. Back row l to r: Laureen Ringer, Beatty Elvin, Renee Bartram, Mary Flatt. Front row l to r: Audrey Townsend, Doreen Wingrove, Freda Wicks.

The 2005 excavation on Browick Road

This work by the Norfolk Archaeology Unit confirmed that Browick or Brathwayte is located in an ancient landscape that has been settled and farmed for thousands of years. The site lies in a small valley in the base of which is a drainage ditch and hedgerow. The ditch is part of a complex which drains into the Tiffey 350 metres to the south west.

The earliest activity was from 3,600 to 3,000 BC and consisted of a probable water course, pits, ditches and Neolithic pottery. The Bronze Age 3,000 – 1800 BC is represented by pottery and worked flint and a pot-boiler mound. These were flints which had been heated in the fire and then put in a cooking pot to heat the contents.

The late Iron Age 300-100 BC is indicated by ditches, pits, pots and postholes. In the Romano-British period, 43-410 AD, ditches, pits and a probable timber built structure were found. The early to mid Saxon period 410-650 AD, produced a hearth or oven, pottery and north of the hearth, a probable sunken featured building.

Moot Hill, near the excavation site, from Browick Road

The Conduit field

In his book on Wymondham Abbey 2007, the late Paul Cattermole wrote of a spring called Estapil near the roundabout on Browick Road which gives access to the bypass. Water from here was collected in a small pond in the conduit field and ran in a lead pipe to the monastery, a wonderful feat of engineering.

Cundyt Close (Conduit)

This close appears in manorial documents. *'In 1536 Robert and William Kett occupy 17 acres of pasture in Brawhite called Cundyt Close granted to them by the Abbot of Wymondham.'* In 1579 Valentine Kett, son of Robert's brother Thomas, gave up Cundyt Close in Brathwayte. His house still stands nearby and is called Banhams Farm House.

Part of the carved mantelpiece from Valentine Kett's house

Finale

This book began with the writings of Thomas Martin the 18th century antiquarian and it will end with him.

His 1722 note confirms the existence of the spring at Browick:

'In an old close by the common lezure (Lizard*) was a conduit brought from a fair spring. The pipes have some of them been lately found there and the close is called Conduit Close in old deeds to this day.'*

235

Acknowledgements

We are grateful to the many people who have written about aspects of Wymondham's history particularly John Wilson, Philip Yaxley, Sheila Spicer, Janet Smith, Mary Garner, Sarah Storey, John Ayton, Richard Fowle, Brenda Garrard, Les King and the late Bruce Wilson and Paul Cattermole. As ever, Wymondham Town Archive and Wymondham Heritage Museum have provided invaluable sources. Others who have given or loaned us useful information and photographs are, the Greene family, Peter Parke, the Gooch family, David Standley, Molly Stone, the late Mr & Mrs R Bunn, Pamela Standley, Colin Proctor, Mrs Scarborough, Michael Marwood, Philip Chapman, Richard and Moira Dean, Janet Finch & Tom Burke, Shirley Foulsham and Mary Standley.
We are indebted to those Wymondham residents who shared their memories back in the 1980s, Mrs Cyril Ayton, Jack Bowden, Tom Turner, 'Tubby' Fulcher, Mr & Mrs John Fulcher, Eva Chapman, Leslie Slaughter, Tom Alderton, Miss Lowe, Dolly Attewell, Mrs Keylock, Reggie Bird, Mrs Knighton, John Lock, George Duffield, Leslie Kerridge, Mrs White, Mrs Bedingfield, Wilfred Coleman, Mrs Smith, Mr WG Wilson, Mrs Fisher, Dick Hewitt and Miss E Carter. Of course, those who talked with them and recorded their conversations - Janis Raynsford, Judy Hawkins and Mr & Mrs Kirkman of the Heritage Society, have performed a valuable service.

Every effort has been made to contact copyright holders for permission to use a photograph where appropriate. Any omission is unintentional and our apologies are offered.

We have tried to be accurate throughout the book. Any shortcomings are unintended and our responsibility.